MAGIC WITH
COINS AND BILLS

MAGIC
WITH COINS
AND BILLS

BILL SEVERN

Illustrations by
Elizabeth Green

David McKay Company, Inc.
New York

COPYRIGHT © 1977 BY Bill Severn
All rights reserved, including the right to reproduce
this book, or parts thereof, in any form, except for
the inclusion of brief quotations in a review.

Library of Congress Cataloging in Publication Data ·

Severn, William.
    Magic with coins and bills.

    Includes index.
    1. Coin tricks.   I. Title.
GV1559.S48   793.8   76-43541

ISBN: 0-679-20380-X

10 9 8 7 6 5 4 3 2
MANUFACTURED IN THE UNITED STATES OF AMERICA

CONTENTS

INTRODUCTION

This is a collection of some of my favorite magic tricks with coins and paper money. I have included many that the beginner should be able to do with a minimum of practice, and for the more advanced magic hobbyist there are novel money magic plots and subtleties of presentation, as well as updated versions of tricks that have become classics of magic.

There are no feats that require unusual skill or expert manipulation, but a section of the book is devoted to basic sleight of hand, clearly explained so that after a little learning even the novice should be able to put it to use for the performance of puzzling magic with coins.

Some of the tricks can be performed almost anywhere, with the coins and bills that you normally carry in your pockets or that you can borrow from someone in your audience. Others require trick coins and bills, other small props, and advance preparation; but everything needed for them can be assembled at home, and simple step-by-step directions are given for putting them together and performing them. There are tricks for showing to small groups of friends, and others for public performance before larger audiences.

The use of play-money bills, instead of real money, is specified for all tricks that involve cutting, marking, gluing, coloring, or otherwise mutilating the bills. Using transparent tape or other temporary adhesives on real coins and bills is not illegal if they can be removed, but it is against the law to deface currency so as to make it "permanently unspendable." Inexpensive play-money bills, available at toy and game counters, come in many varieties, so it is a good idea to shop around to choose those that are well printed on paper of good quality, and in sizes that are somewhat the same as real money. You won't be trying to convince the audience you are using dollar bills; it is enough in these tricks to suggest the use of money.

As with all forms of magic, tricks with coins and bills should be rehearsed not only individually but in sequence. Even a seemingly "impromptu" showing of just a few simple tricks should be well planned in advance, so that you know not only exactly what you are going to do next and how you will do it, but also where everything will be arranged for the whole performance. Otherwise, you may be embarrassed to discover that a pocket you want to be empty is already stuffed with things used in a previous trick, or you may have to fumble around to fish out the things needed and get them into position. Careful planning and rehearsal also give you the confidence that will let you concentrate on the presentation of individual tricks, which should be practiced until you no longer have to think consciously about each secret move you are making.

The basic methods of magic are a common heritage of all magicians. No claim of originality is made for the methods used in the tricks explained here. Although some have been put to new uses, the methods generally are those that have become accepted as standard and practical. Credit for them belongs to a long line of magicians, who through trial and error have worked them out over the years.

The secrets of tricks, especially of good tricks, are often far more simple than the audience imagines. But for the magician, knowing how a trick is done is not at all the same as knowing how to do it, how to present it interestingly and entertainingly. It may be fun to be fooled, but it certainly is a lot more fun for those who are watching if they are entertained while they are being fooled.

Good presentation is the real secret of magical entertainment, and it comes only through practice, by gradually learning how to please your audiences with what you do. It cannot be taught by any book; it grows out of the personality and style of each performer, and from experience. But I hope that the routines in this book may at least suggest how the secrets of magic can be built into presentations that clothe mere "tricks" with real entertainment.

1

HAND MAGIC WITH COINS

While it is true that advanced sleight of hand with coins requires long practice and much skill, there are a dozen or so basic moves that are comparatively easy to learn. Once learned, they equip the magician to perform many tricks with just his hands and the ordinary coins that are available. They also provide him with a know-how that can be applied to more elaborate tricks.

Some practice is needed, but that is so with all kinds of magic. For simple hand magic with coins, the most important thing to be learned is not intricate manipulation, but a knack of handling the coins naturally and easily. You also need to do a bit of acting to be convincing.

What is sleight of hand?

Sleight of hand is really just pretending. You pretend to catch a coin at your fingertips, to vanish it, to make it fly invisibly from hand to hand, to magically change a penny to a dime or change a quarter to a half-dollar. You put on an act. Like any actor playing a role, you pretend to be a magician.

1

What you secretly do with your hands is only part of that act. Like the backstage props in a theater that are hidden from view, sleight of hand is the hidden part of magic, but it is not the whole show. It must be done well enough so that the audience is not aware of it, but what you should always try to keep in mind is what you are *pretending* to do.

What makes magic entertaining to watch and fun to perform is the way you use its secrets to create illusion. You secretly do one thing while you pretend—with your hands, your voice, your eyes, the expression on your face—to do something else. As you learn the moves that are about to be explained, think of the *effect* that you want them to have, what it is that you want your audience to believe.

All of magic is theater. Even when you do something as simple as showing a friend a penny in your hand and then making it disappear, you are putting on a little theatrical performance. You don't have to make a big thing of it. In fact, the more casually you seem to do it, the more surprising it may be. But you do have to act it out, not just go through the fingering.

If you move one hand away from the other, people usually will look at the hand that is moving. If you look down at one hand instead of the other, they will look where you look. That is all part of what magicians call *misdirection,* doing things to lead people's thoughts and attention to what you are pretending and away from the real secret of the trick. The success of magic depends much more on skillful misdirection than any secret moves and devices.

But a lot of it comes naturally. Most people are apt to think in terms of what they would normally expect to see, unless you give them some reason to think otherwise. If the palm of your hand is toward the floor, they tend to think there is nothing in it, because normally anything in your hand would fall out. By habit of thought, they assume that an upside-down hand is an empty hand—unless you hold it in a stiff, unnatural position that makes them take a second look.

A good general rule for hand magic is to manipulate the hands as slightly as necessary to accomplish whatever you are pretending to do with them. If you are hiding a coin in one hand while you pretend to put it into the other hand, the more naturally you can do it, the more convincing it will be.

The object is not to demonstrate how clever you are at hiding the coin by wiggling your fingers around or showing your hand this way or that, but simply to keep from arousing suspicion that you are doing anything "tricky" with it at all. If you go through a lot of elaborate manipulation to try to prove that you aren't hiding something, you may only call attention to the fact that you are.

Practice and rehearsal

Watching yourself in a mirror can help with practicing, but it may also make you self-conscious when you are first trying to learn a new move, so that you become fussy, tense, or timid. Probably the best way to begin is to read the directions and then just go about trying it. Run through it a few times, fumbles and all, until you think you can do it fairly well. Then stand before a mirror and watch yourself as an audience would. Watch the angles, correct the faults, and try it again without the mirror.

If you have a coin palmed in your hand, try doing other things with the fingers of that hand. With the coin concealed, pick things up, carry them, put them down. Try using those fingers to turn the pages of a magazine, to open a bureau drawer, to button your jacket. You can have fun making a sort of game of it, to get used to the natural handling of things while you keep the coin hidden.

But as you practice, also remember that the move itself is only part of the act of pretending. Put it to use in some trick you intend to do and go through the whole trick just as if an audience were really watching. Speak to the people in your imaginary audience, look up at them, smile, look down

at the hand you want them to look at. Do it as an actor
would rehearse a part in a play.

What coins to use

Most of these basic moves can be done with ordinary
coins of any size, but the larger ones are easiest to hold and
to get into place. For the person with hands of average size,
the best coins to use for learning are half-dollars. They are
big enough to grip properly and have good weight and
milled edges, which helps in handling them. If your hands
are rather small, you may want to begin with quarters.
Once you are confident that you can do a move fairly well,
try using coins of all sizes.

Remember that coins are light. You don't have to grip
them forcefully, squeeze them tight, or hold on to them for
dear life. Gently does it!

THE FINGER-PALM

The purpose

Finger-palming is used to hold coins or other small things
in the partly closed fingers of either hand so that the back of
the hand hides them from view of the audience. It has many
uses and leaves the hands and fingers fairly free to pick up
and hold other things. Finger-palming looks very natural
and is probably the easiest method of palming.

The handling

When a coin is properly finger-palmed, it is held at the
base of the partly closed second and third fingers, between
the middle joints of those fingers and the edge of the palm.

But to understand why the finger-palm looks so naturally
deceptive, first try this, without any coin in your hands:
Stand in front of a mirror and drop your hands to your sides,
so they hang loosely as they usually do when you're not
using them. You will see that your fingers normally curl
inward because of the natural curve of the backs of your
relaxed hands.

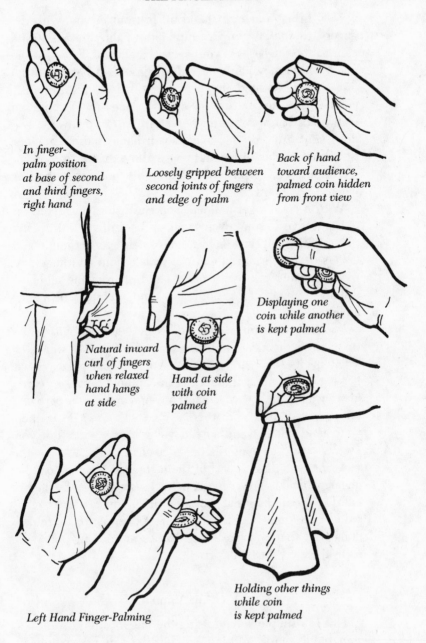

In finger-palm position at base of second and third fingers, right hand

Loosely gripped between second joints of fingers and edge of palm

Back of hand toward audience, palmed coin hidden from front view

Natural inward curl of fingers when relaxed hand hangs at side

Hand at side with coin palmed

Displaying one coin while another is kept palmed

Left Hand Finger-Palming

Holding other things while coin is kept palmed

Now bring your right hand up in front of you, with the fingers still loosely cupped, and hold it palm upward. Rest a coin flat on the bases of your second and third fingers, at the place where they join your palm. Close your hand slightly, just enough to hold the coin there between the middle joints of those fingers and the edge of the palm. Keeping the coin held that way, turn your hand palm downward and drop your arm so your hand again hangs loosely at your side. Look in the mirror and you will see that with the coin hidden in your fingers, your hand still looks as natural as when it was empty.

With a coin finger-palmed, you can bring your hand up in front of you, palm toward you, and gesture with it freely, point with your first finger, even snap your thumb and fingers if you wish. You can use your thumb and fingers to pick things up from your other hand or from the table, to display another coin, to hold up a handkerchief, a pencil, or an envelope.

You can pick up a small glass and hold it with your thumb and fingers around the sides, or hold a bag, a box, or a hat by its top rear edge with your fingers partly down inside and thumb at the back. You can hold a pack of cards in your hand, or put your hand on someone's arm, pat your pockets, and reach into them. What you *can't* do is open your hand out flat and spread your fingers wide, but you usually would have no reason to do that.

A single coin or several of them stacked together can be finger-palmed in either hand, or various coins can be finger-palmed in both hands at the same time. You can also finger-palm such things as a bottle cap, poker chip, or folded dollar bill that you may want to use in combination with coins for some particular trick.

Pick-up Vanish

This is a simple way of using the finger-palm to vanish a coin, but as simple as it is, it can be effective if done quickly

THE FINGER-PALM—II

GESTURING

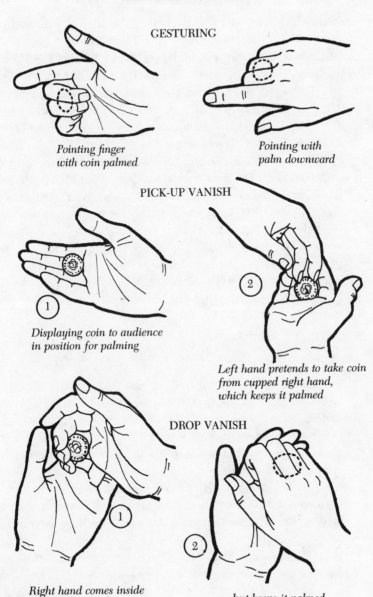

Pointing finger
with coin palmed

Pointing with
palm downward

PICK-UP VANISH

Displaying coin to audience
in position for palming

Left hand pretends to take coin
from cupped right hand,
which keeps it palmed

DROP VANISH

Right hand comes inside
cupped left fingers and
pretends to drop coin . . .

but keeps it palmed
as hands draw apart

and boldly. The way it looks is that you show a coin resting on the fingers of your right hand. You pick it up with your other hand and throw it high into the air, and it vanishes.

Place the coin on your right hand, at the base of the two middle fingers in a position to finger-palm it, and lower that hand a little to display it there. Bring your left hand down from above, fingertips downward, as if to pick up the coin between the thumb and fingers.

Pass the left-hand fingers across the coin, pinching thumb and fingers together as though taking it, and lift your left hand straight up. As you do that, turn your right hand slightly toward you and immediately let it drop to your side with the coin finger-palmed.

Look at your left hand, make a tossing motion as you pretend to throw the coin high into the air, open the hand wide so it is seen to be empty, and look up into the air as though following the flight of the coin as it vanishes.

Drop Vanish

Like many moves with coins, this finger-palm vanish is based on the notion that to an audience an upside-down hand is an empty hand. Watchers see your right hand turn over as it apparently drops a coin into your left hand, which closes around it, but when the left hand opens a moment later the coin is gone.

Start by showing the coin lying on your right hand. Bounce it flat once or twice so it slides to rest over the base of your two middle fingers in a position for finger-palming it.

Hold out your left hand, fingertips toward the audience and cupped upward slightly. Turn your right hand over toward you, finger-palming the coin as you bring the hand palm downward inside the cupped fingers of the left hand as if to drop the coin into it. Without pausing, draw your hands apart, closing the left fingers as if they held the coin.

Lift that hand a little as you look at it and point to it with the first finger of your palm-downward right hand.

This should all be done casually, as though you merely showed a coin with one hand, dropped it into the other, and closed that hand around it. Thrust the closed left hand forward slightly and let your right hand fall loosely to your side. Slowly open your left hand and show that the coin has vanished.

THE THUMB-PALM

The purpose

Thumb-palming is secretly holding a coin in the crotch of the thumb so that the coin is hidden from view when the back of the hand is toward those who are watching. The coin is clipped flat under the thumb below the base of the first finger and is held there at the extreme edge of the palm by the pressure of the side of the thumb.

The thumb-palm is most often used for the production or vanish of a coin at the fingertips, for quickly palming a coin while pretending to throw it into the other hand, or for palming it while seeming to drop it into something such as a hat, a bag, or a box. The fingers are free and can even be spread apart, and the hand looks from the back as though it couldn't be holding anything.

The thumb-palm is not difficult but requires some practice to do casually and naturally and to avoid rapid jerking movements of the hand while getting the coin back and forth from the fingers into the crotch of the thumb.

The handling

To understand where the coin is held when it is in thumb-palm position, first try this: Hold your right hand palm upward in front of you, fingertips toward the front and thumb toward the right. Lift your thumb up and a little to the right, to get it out of the way for a moment.

Lay a coin flat on the extreme right edge of the hand,

THE THUMB-PALM—I

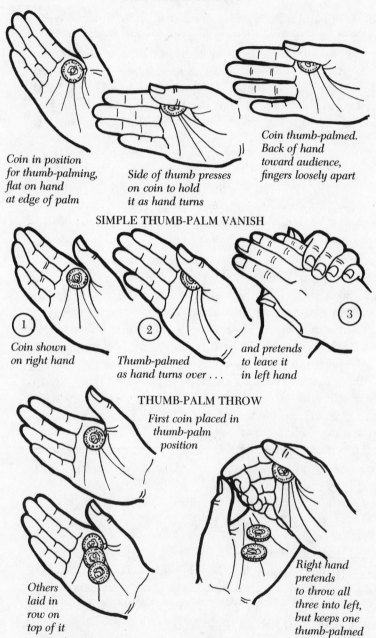

Coin in position
for thumb-palming,
flat on hand
at edge of palm

Side of thumb presses
on coin to hold
it as hand turns

Coin thumb-palmed.
Back of hand
toward audience,
fingers loosely apart

SIMPLE THUMB-PALM VANISH

1 Coin shown
on right hand

2 Thumb-palmed
as hand turns over . . .

3 and pretends
to leave it
in left hand

THUMB-PALM THROW

First coin placed in
thumb-palm
position

Others
laid in
row on
top of it

Right hand
pretends
to throw all
three into left,
but keeps one
thumb-palmed

10

below your lifted thumb, so it rests on the hand between the fork of the thumb and the base of the first finger. Now bring the side of the thumb down against the right half of the coin and press against it to hold the coin between the thumb and the edge of the hand.

Keep your thumb and fingers as they are and turn your whole hand so the palm is toward you, thumb at the top, fingertips pointing to the left. The coin is now thumb-palmed, hidden from front view by the back of the hand. You can bring the hand palm downward to your other hand or to a table, drop the hand loosely to your side, point with it, or move it around freely, as long as you don't turn it with the palm directly toward the audience. Coins can be thumb-palmed with either hand.

A common mistake in thumb-palming is to hold the hand out stiffly, with the back of it flat and the fingers spread wide apart. There is a temptation to do that to "prove" you have nothing in your fingers, but it looks awkward and unnatural. Just hold the hand in a normally relaxed way, with the fingers slightly apart, so there is a natural curving of the back of the hand and the fingers. The tip of the thumb and part of the side of it should show above the top of the hand, but the coin should be well within the hand so none of it shows.

Simple Thumb-Palm Vanish

Show a coin with your left hand and place it on your upturned right hand so that it rests near the edge of the hand beneath the base of the first finger. Display it there and hold out your left hand, palm upward.

Turn your right hand over, palm downward, to bring it above the left hand, and as you do that just press the side of the right thumb against the coin to hold it. Continue to bring your right hand down into the left, as if dropping the coin, and start to close your left fingers loosely up around your right fingers as you draw your hands apart.

Lift your closed left hand a little, as though taking the dropped coin, and let your right hand fall to your side with the coin thumb-palmed. Look at your closed left hand, slowly open the fingers, and show that the coin has vanished.

Thumb-Palm Throw

In much the same way as the vanish, you can show several coins in one hand and pretend to throw them all together into the other hand, but really hold back one of them by keeping it thumb-palmed. This throw can be used in various ways, such as pretending to make one of several coins fly invisibly from hand to hand.

Show three coins, for example, and lay them in a row across the palm of your right hand so that one of the three is at the edge of the hand in a position for thumb-palming it. Hold out your left hand and turn your right hand palm downward over it to throw the coins from hand to hand, but squeeze the side of your right thumb to the coin positioned under it and keep that one thumb-palmed as the others fall into your left hand.

Immediately close your left hand around the coins it catches and jingle them in that hand as you drop your right hand to your side. The sound of the two coins clinking together in your left hand is deceptive and adds to the illusion that you threw all three from hand to hand.

To make a simple trick of it, pretend to throw the three from your right hand to your left, but keep one thumb-palmed and drop your right hand to your side. Hold out your closed left hand, which supposedly contains all three. Now bring up your right hand with its back toward the audience, turn it palm downward, and slowly close the fingers. Hold both closed hands in front of you and command one coin to fly invisibly from your left hand to your right. Open the left hand and drop its two coins on the table, showing that the hand is otherwise empty. Then open your right hand and drop out the coin that was thumb-palmed.

Fingertip Vanish

If you want to use the thumb-palm to make a coin held by the fingertips visibly seem to vanish, you have to secretly move it from the fingers into the crotch of the thumb to grip it there. This is done by quickly closing the hand and opening it out again. Here is how to position the coin in the fingers to do that:

Hold your right hand in front of you, palm toward you, thumb at the top and fingers pointed toward the left. Turn a coin so that its face and back are horizontal. Now hold it clipped flat between the sides of your first and second fingers, near the tips of them. As much of the coin as possible should be visible beyond the tips of the fingers, but with enough kept between the fingers to grip it securely.

That is how you display the coin at your fingertips before thumb-palming it. When performing, you can first display it in another position and then move it into the finger clip to hold it in view, or else show it first with the other hand and quickly clip it between your fingertips to show it.

To thumb-palm it so as to make it seem to vanish from your fingertips as you throw it into the air, start by showing it clipped between your fingers, with the back of your hand toward the audience. With a slight wave of your hand, pretend to throw the coin out to the left. As you make the throwing motion, close your hand so the fingers curl inward to bring the coin back into the crotch of your thumb. Press your thumb against it to hold it in the regular thumb-palm position. When it is securely held by your thumb, straighten out your fingers again.

With a little practice, this can be done quite rapidly, but more important, it should be done smoothly. The rapid closing and opening of the fingers while the hand is moving seems a natural part of the throwing motion and won't be

THE THUMB-PALM—II

FINGERTIP VANISHES AND PRODUCTIONS
VANISH

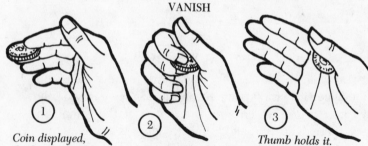

1 Coin displayed, flat between sides of first and second fingers

2 Fingers close quickly to bring coin into crotch of thumb

3 Thumb holds it. As fingers quickly open out again, coin vanishes

PRODUCTION

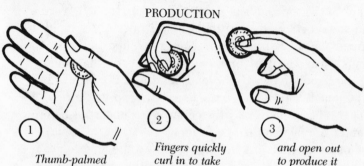

1 Thumb-palmed coin hidden from front view

2 Fingers quickly curl in to take it from crotch of thumb . . .

3 and open out to produce it at fingertips

THUMB-PALM DROP

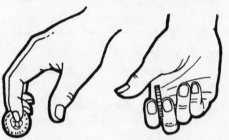

Fingers show coin and pretend to put it into a hat

With hand partly inside, fingers curl to grip coin in crotch of thumb

Hand brought out with back to audience. Seems to have left coin in hat

noticed if you do it without hesitating. All the audience really sees is that one moment the coin was at your fingertips and now they are empty.

Fingertip Production

To produce a coin at the fingertips, you use the same handling as for vanishing it, but in reverse. Instead of secretly moving the coin into the crotch of your thumb, you take it from there.

Start with a coin palmed in the crotch of your thumb in the regular thumb-palm position. Hold up your hand with its back to the audience to show the fingers empty. With a little waving motion, reach out toward the left as if to catch an invisible coin from the air. As you do that, quickly close the hand, curl the fingers inward to the crotch of the thumb, grip the coin so it is clipped between your first and second fingers, and open out your hand to show it at your fingertips.

The production and vanish are often combined, as in the classic trick of magically producing a number of coins from the air and collecting them in a hat or metal bucket. A full routine for that is explained in the section *"Catching Coins from the Air"* in chapter 4 of this book.

Thumb-Palm Drop

You can thumb-palm a coin while seeming to drop it from your right-hand fingers into a hat, a bag, a handkerchief, or something else that is being held by your left hand. For example, hold out a hat by its brim with your left hand, and display the coin as before at the fingertips of your right hand. Pretend to drop the coin into the hat with a slight throwing motion as you put your hand a little way down inside the hat. Quickly close your fingers to thumb-palm the coin, and immediately open them out and remove your hand, apparently having left the coin in the hat.

PUSHES, PIVOTS, AND DROPS

The purpose

These are ways of holding a coin to display it at your fingertips so that you can then secretly push it, pivot it, or let it drop out of sight behind your fingers. They are usually used to vanish a coin, to pretend to take it from one hand with the other, or for switching coins, substituting one for another.

The handling

Each of these pushes, pivots, and drops is handled in a slightly different way, but most of them start with the coin displayed in much the same way at the fingertips.

To understand the basic positioning, start by bringing your right hand up in front of you, with the fingertips pointing straight up toward the ceiling, palm toward you, back of the hand toward the audience, and all four fingers held together. Place the bottom edge of a coin flat against the inside tips of your first and second fingers and press the tip of your thumb against the back of the coin to hold it so that most of the coin shows from the front above the tips of the fingers.

That is how it is first displayed to the audience. But with the coin that way at the fingertips, you can turn the hand itself in other directions. For some of these moves, you won't want to keep your hand with the fingers pointed upward. You may hold it with the fingers pointed toward the left or down to the floor. In any case, and with either hand, the coin is held in view between the tips of the fingers at the front and the thumb at the back.

You may pick the coin up from the table between your thumb and fingertips to show it, take it from your pocket or your other hand to hold it that way, or first show it lying on the palm of your hand and push it to your fingertips with your thumb to display it.

PUSHES, PIVOTS, AND DROPS—I

Displaying coin between thumb and fingertips.
Hand turned in various directions

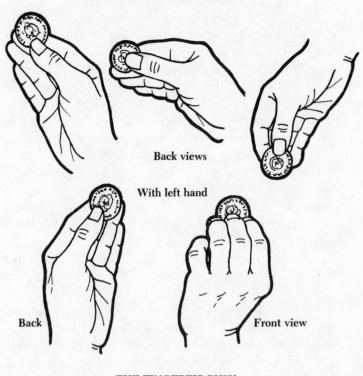

Back views

With left hand

Back

Front view

THE FINGERTIP PUSH

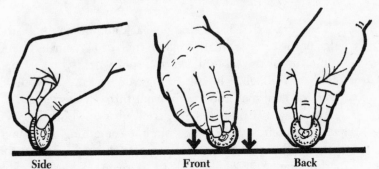

Side

Front

Back

Fingertip Push

With this, you simply press the visible edge of the coin against something, which pushes it out of sight behind your fingers. Let's say, for example, that you want to pretend to push a coin through the top of a table. Stand behind the table and pick up the coin with your right hand to hold it near its edge between your thumb and the tips of your fingers. With the coin gripped that way, turn your hand downward, so the fingertips point toward the table and the backs of the fingers are toward the audience.

Bring your hand down until the bottom edge of the coin touches the table top and hold the coin in view there for a moment. Then, as if pushing the coin through the table, push your hand straight down so your fingers cover the coin and the tips of them touch the table. Pushing down automatically slides the coin up between your thumb and fingers so that it is concealed from front view behind your fingers.

Without changing the position of your thumb and fingers, which still hold the hidden coin, lift your hand a little and quickly move it 6 to 8 inches to the right. Hold it there an instant, to create the illusion that since the coin is no longer visible at your fingertips it must have been pushed into the table.

Then draw that hand straight back and down under the edge of the table, and at the same time bring your left hand to the top of the table to rub the spot where you "pushed the coin through." Finally bring your right hand out to show the coin that apparently went through the table.

The fingertip push is not a trick in itself, but merely a way of pretending to push a coin into something or through some solid object as part of some trick that you may be performing. You might use it to seem to push a coin through your leg, arm, head, the back of your other hand, or the side or bottom of a box or cup in which you have a duplicate coin hidden.

The Push Vanish

This is an easy way of vanishing a coin by using the fingertip push. What you seem to do is show a coin at the fingertips of one hand and put it into the palm of the other hand, which closes around it and turns over as though holding the coin. When you open that hand a moment later, the coin is gone.

What you really do is push the bottom edge of the coin against the palm of your other hand so it slides up behind your fingers and is hidden. The closing and turning of your other hand helps draw attention away from the hand hiding the coin.

Start by holding up a coin to show it between the thumb and fingertips of the right hand. Bring your left hand palm upward in front of you, with the tips of its fingers toward the audience, and turn your right hand palm downward so the coin it is holding is directly above the left hand.

Now bring your right hand down to your left until the bottom edge of the coin is touching your left palm and hold it there a moment so the coin is clearly seen. Begin to close your left-hand fingers, and as you do, press the edge of the coin against your palm so it slides up into your right-hand fingers and is hidden behind them. As you continue to close your left hand into a fist as though holding the coin, lift your right hand away and out a few inches to the right so the audience can see that the coin is no longer at your fingertips. Immediately turn your left fist over, thumb downward, with a little forward thrust of that hand, and at the same time let your right hand drop to your side with the coin concealed.

In all of this, the position of your right thumb and fingers doesn't change at all. You just push the edge of the coin

THE PUSH VANISH—Side views

THE PIVOT VANISH

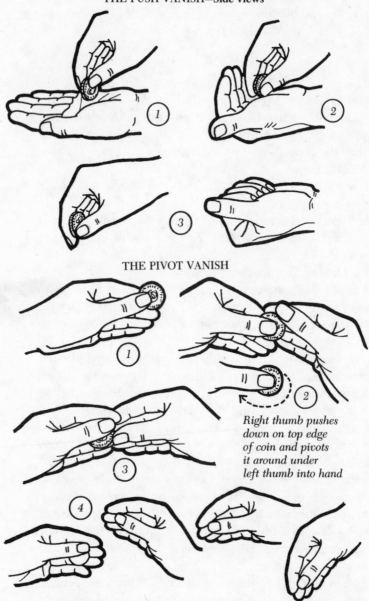

Right thumb pushes
down on top edge
of coin and pivots
it around under
left thumb into hand

against your left palm, keep your thumb and fingers in the same position as you lift your hand away, hold it out to the right a moment, and then let that hand drop to your side, while the left hand keeps moving and turning to attract attention.

Finally look at your closed left fist as you hold it out in front of you. Slowly open your left hand, turn it upward to show that the coin has vanished, and let that hand drop to its side.

The Pivot Vanish

In this method of pretending to take a coin from one hand with the other to vanish it, the hand displaying the coin at its fingertips does almost nothing at all. Its thumb merely acts as a pivot so that when the thumb of the other hand touches the edge of the coin it gives it a tiny downward turn that hides it from view. The whole thing is quick, natural-looking, and easy to do.

Pick up a coin and hold it at its edge between the thumb and the tips of the first two fingers of the left hand, with that hand in front of you so the fingers are toward the right and the back of the hand is toward the audience. Reach over with the right hand, palm toward you, as if to take the coin between its thumb and fingers. Bring the hands together so the right-hand fingers go to the front with their tips close to the knuckles of the left hand. This brings your right thumb to the top edge of the coin.

As your right thumb touches the top of the coin just push down on it gently so it pivots around under the tip of your left thumb and down behind the left fingers. The left hand doesn't move at all and the only movement of your right hand is the tiny downward push of the thumb as it touches the top edge of the coin.

Keep your left hand as it is and draw your right hand away to the right as though taking the coin. The backs of both hands are still toward the audience. It should look as though you just showed the coin at the fingertips of your left hand and casually took it with your right hand.

As you lift your right hand a little, let your left hand drop naturally to your side. Then open your right hand and show that the coin has vanished. While you do that, your left thumb can easily slide the hidden coin into a finger-palm position inside the left hand, so that you can then use that hand more freely with the coin concealed.

Fingertip Drop

This is still another way of secretly keeping a coin in one hand while pretending to take it with the other. Again the hand displaying the coin seems not to move at all, and in this trick the coin really hides itself. Under the cover of your other hand, it drops from your fingertips because of its own weight and slides right down into position for finger-palming it.

Start by holding up the coin to show it between the thumb and fingertips of the left hand, with that hand held upright so the fingers point toward the ceiling and the back of it is toward the audience. The hand should be held at about waist level.

With the right hand, reach over as if to take the coin, bringing the tips of the right fingers in front of the upright fingertips of the left hand and the right thumb just in back of the coin.

As your right hand screens the coin from front view for an instant, lift your left thumb to release the coin and let it slide down from your fingertips. It will drop by its own weight and slide down against the inside of your fingers to the base of them in finger-palm position.

Keeping your left hand as it is, take your right hand away as if holding the coin and close the fingers into a loose fist as though the coin were in it. As you look at your lifting right hand, let your left hand drop to your side with the finger-palmed coin. With a little rubbing motion of your right-

FINGERTIP DROP

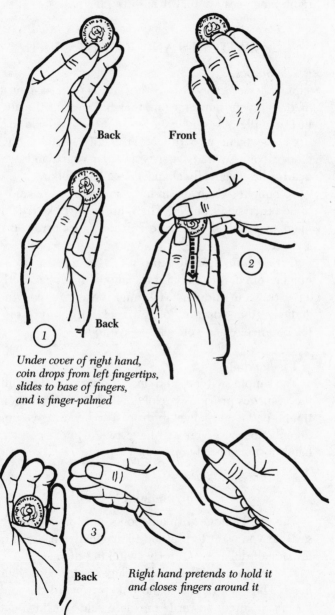

Back   Front

Back

(1)   (2)

Under cover of right hand,
coin drops from left fingertips,
slides to base of fingers,
and is finger-palmed

(3)

Back   *Right hand pretends to hold it*
and closes fingers around it

hand fingers, pretend to vanish the coin, and then open the right hand to show that it has disappeared.

SWITCHES AND FALSE COUNTS

The purpose

Switches are ways of secretly exchanging a coin that is hidden in your hand for one that is shown to the audience. For example, you might show a quarter and seem to drop it from one hand into the other, really switching it for a hidden coin, so that when you open your hand again the quarter has magically changed to a half-dollar.

You might switch a coin for a bottle cap, a poker chip, or some other small object. There are also tricks that depend upon switching a duplicate coin for one borrowed from a spectator.

False counts usually are used to transfer a counted number of coins from hand to hand while you secretly keep an extra coin hidden. You might want to convince the audience that you are doing a trick with only three coins, for instance, when you really have four.

The handling

The simple switches and false counts given here all make use of moves previously explained, such as the finger-palm, thumb-palm, and fingertip drop. The handling is somewhat different because you will have two or more coins in your hands instead of only one.

Finger-Palm Switch

This can be done with any coins, but for explanation let's say that you want to pretend to magically change a quarter into a half-dollar by secretly switching them.

You start with a half-dollar finger-palmed in your right hand. The back of that hand is kept toward the audience, fingers pointed toward the left and curling naturally inward, with the concealed half-dollar held in the usual

SWITCHES AND FALSE COUNTS—I

FINGER-PALM SWITCH

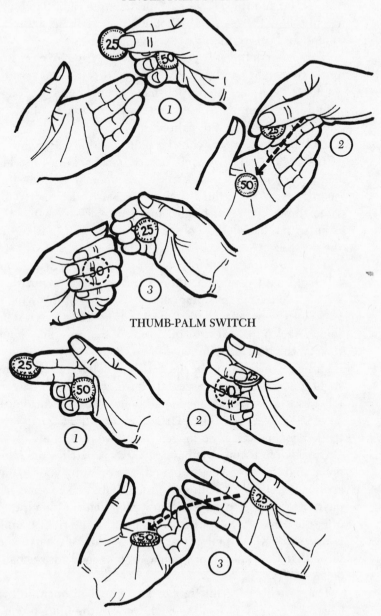

THUMB-PALM SWITCH

finger-palm position between the middle joints and base of the second and third fingers. With the same right hand, you openly show the quarter by holding it in view between the thumb and tips of the first two fingers.

Turn your left hand palm upward in front of you and bring your right hand down over it and toss the quarter into your left hand. Close your left-hand fingers quickly around it and then open them again and lower that hand a little to show the quarter on the palm of it.

Pick up the quarter with the thumb and first two fingers of the right hand, and once more toss it back into the left hand, close the left hand, and then open it to show the quarter. Now for a third time you seem to do exactly the same thing, but on the third toss you secretly switch the coins so the half-dollar goes into your left hand instead of the quarter.

This third time, as before, pick up the quarter from your left hand with your right thumb and first two fingers, and without hesitating make the same movement of throwing it back into your left hand. But this time slide your right thumb back a little against the inside of the right first finger to keep the quarter there, and open the rest of your fingers slightly to throw out the hidden half-dollar instead. The slight opening of your second, third, and fourth fingers releases the finger-palmed half-dollar and also almost automatically hides the quarter behind those partly extended fingers so it is no longer visible from in front.

Quickly close your left hand again as it catches the half-dollar and this time keep it closed. As you draw your hands apart, move your right thumb inside that hand to slide the quarter into finger-palm position so that you can then point or gesture freely. Only a tiny movement of the right thumb is necessary to do that. Finally, open your left hand and show that the quarter has magically changed into a half-dollar.

The switch really amounts to no more than opening the fingers of your right hand enough to drop the hidden coin, but the moves should all blend into one simple action of seeming to toss a coin from one hand to the other. What takes a little practice is the timing, so that you don't do it too slowly or too quickly, but with the same even speed each time. The movement should look the same no matter which coin is thrown.

Thumb-Palm Switch

This serves the same purpose of showing one coin and secretly switching it for another. Let's suppose again that you wish to show a quarter and secretly switch it for a half-dollar.

Start with the half-dollar finger-palmed in your right hand. With that hand, openly display the quarter and then hold it clipped flat between the sides of your first and second fingers, just as you would if you were about to vanish the quarter from your fingertips by thumb-palming it.

Turn your left hand palm upward in front of you and bring your right hand palm downward to it, as if to drop the quarter into your left hand. But what you really do is thumb-palm the quarter with your right hand. As you bring your right hand down, quickly close its fingers so as to curl them in and leave the quarter in the crotch of your thumb, and then quickly open your fingers out again. The opening out of your fingers releases the half-dollar so that it drops into your left hand instead of the quarter.

You simply thumb-palm the quarter as if you had no half-dollar finger-palmed in that hand, and the half-dollar will drop out by itself as you reopen your fingers.

Shut your left-hand fingers around the half-dollar and take your right hand away. The quarter is now safely thumb-palmed in your right hand, which looks empty from the back, since you can hold it naturally with the fingers slightly apart. When you are ready to reveal the change, open your left hand and show that the half-dollar is there instead of the quarter.

The Glass Switch

This is almost the same as the thumb-palm switch, but instead of dropping the switched coin into your left hand, you drop it into a drinking glass. You can use this technique to switch a duplicate coin for one you borrow from someone in the audience, so that you seem to leave the borrowed coin in full view in the glass that you put on your table. That gives you secret possession of the borrowed coin for use in whatever trick you may be doing.

You will need an ordinary drinking glass and a coin of the same denomination as the one you intend to borrow. A quarter is probably better to use than a half-dollar, because people are more likely to have quarters with them.

Have your own quarter finger-palmed in your right hand, which hangs naturally at your side, and have the glass on your table. Ask if one of the spectators will let you borrow a quarter. When one is offered, ask the person to please look at it and read the date aloud so everyone will remember it.

While he is doing that, pick up the glass near the bottom of it with your right hand, between the thumb and first two fingers, and with the back of the hand toward those who are watching. Holding the glass in that hand for a moment gives the impression that the hand is otherwise empty and helps to conceal the finger-palmed coin.

As you step toward the spectator, transfer the glass to your left hand. Reach out with your palm-downward right hand and take the offered quarter between your thumb and first two fingers.

Hold the coin in view clipped between your first two fingers in a position for thumb-palming it. Immediately bring your right hand to the top of the glass as if to drop the borrowed quarter into it, but quickly close and then reopen your fingers to thumb-palm the borrowed one and let your own quarter fall into the glass instead. Shake the glass with your left hand to rattle the coin inside it and let your right hand drop to your side.

SWITCHES AND FALSE COUNTS—II

THE GLASS SWITCH

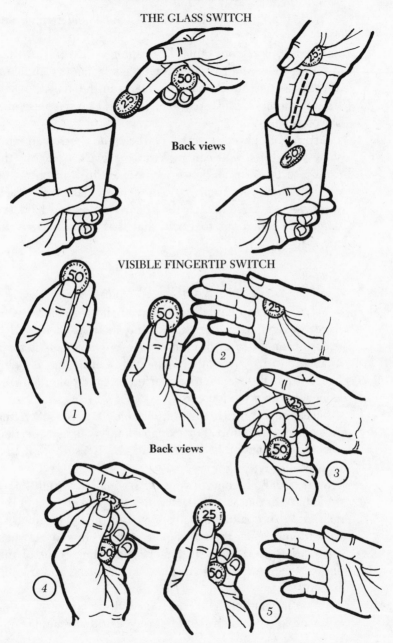

Back views

VISIBLE FINGERTIP SWITCH

Back views

With the glass still in your left hand, hold it high and rattle the coin in it again as you turn slightly toward the left and step back to your table. Keep the glass in full view, put it on the table, and leave it there. As far as the audience knows, the borrowed quarter remains in the glass, but you have it thumb-palmed in your right hand to make use of it as you wish.

After you have secretly planted the borrowed coin somewhere else, you can pick up the glass, pour out the duplicate that the audience assumes is still the borrowed one, and vanish it. Then you can seem to make it reappear wherever you have hidden the borrowed one and have the date on it called out to verify that it is the same one the spectator gave you.

Visible Fingertip Switch

What seems to happen is that you show a coin at your fingertips and pass your other hand in front of it, and it visibly changes to a different coin. As you touch it for a moment with your other hand, a half-dollar at your fingertips might change to a quarter, to a red poker chip, or from silver to a foreign coin of copper.

There is no intricate manipulation. It is based on the simple fingertip drop. For explanation, we'll suppose that you want to show a half-dollar and visibly "shrink" it to a quarter.

Start with both coins in your otherwise empty right-hand pocket. With that hand, reach into your pocket and get the quarter thumb-palmed by pushing it up into the crotch of your thumb. Take the half-dollar so it is clipped between the sides of your first two fingers and bring it out of the pocket to show it, with the back of the hand toward the audience.

Hold out your left hand, drop the half-dollar on the palm of it, and let your right hand fall to your side for a moment.

Lower the left hand a little to display the coin, and let the coin slide out to the fingers so the thumb can push it into position for the fingertip drop. Lift that hand with its back toward the audience so the fingertips point upward and the half-dollar is held in view between the fingertips at the front and thumb at the back.

Bring your right hand up with its fingertips toward the left so it goes horizontally across in front of your upright left-hand fingers, touching against the outside tips of them. As your right hand screens the left for a moment, let the half-dollar drop and slide down into the base of your left-hand fingers, ready for finger-palming.

Continue to move your right hand across horizontally until the thumb-palmed quarter comes into your left thumb and fingertips. Close your left thumb on the bottom edge of the quarter to hold it between thumb and fingertips just as the half-dollar was held. Then lower your right hand to reveal the change. The half-dollar that was displayed at your left fingertips magically has changed to a quarter.

The whole thing really amounts to letting the half-dollar slide down into your left-hand fingers as your right hand moves across in front of them to leave the thumb-palmed quarter in place of it. The passing across and lowering of the right hand should be done in one continuous motion, with the left hand not changing position at all.

Hold the quarter as it is for a moment, so everyone can see the change that has taken place. Then casually show your right hand empty, take the quarter with it, and let your left hand fall to your side, finger-palming the half-dollar.

Thumb-Palm False Count

This is a way of using the previously explained thumb-palm throw to convince spectators you have only two coins when you really have three, or three when you really have four. It is a move that serves many purposes. The counted-out coins are fairly shown, first in one hand and then the other, yet you are able to keep an extra coin hidden.

Let's say that you want to show only two half-dollars and that you have reached the point in some trick where you have a third half-dollar thumb-palmed in your right hand. Place the two that you want the audience to see on the palm of your left hand, spread out so one of them is close to the edge of that palm, in position for thumb-palming.

Lower your left hand a little and hold it slightly toward the left to show the two coins to the spectators at that side. Then, with a slight inward swing toward the right, turn your left hand palm downward as if to drop the two coins into your right hand, which turns upward to take them. But as you turn your left hand over, close the side of that thumb on the coin beneath it so that only one of the coins you have just shown falls into your right hand when the hands touch together.

Lift your right thumb to release the extra coin it was holding and move your right hand out toward the right, to show the spectators at that side the two coins that are now lying on your right hand. You are really showing them the one coin that fell from your left hand and the one that was already in your right hand. It looks as though you are showing the same two after having dropped them from one hand to the other, but you now have an extra coin thumb-palmed in your left hand.

This should be done in a natural, unhurried way, by bringing the left hand down over the right as if to casually transfer the two coins from hand to hand so as to show them clearly, first to the spectators at one side and then to those at the other side.

The moves can be made in reverse, of course, by starting with an extra coin thumb-palmed in your left hand and finishing with one hidden in your right hand, if some particular trick requires that. The handling is the same if you want to show three coins when you really have four.

THUMB-PALM FALSE COUNT

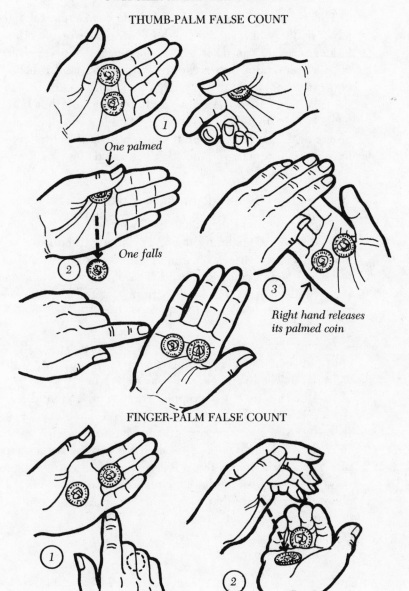

One palmed

One falls

Right hand releases
its palmed coin

FINGER-PALM FALSE COUNT

This also can be used to show that you have a quarter and a half-dollar, while you keep a duplicate of one or the other hidden. Or you can do it with a copper and a silver coin, with a coin and a bottle cap, or with a coin and a poker chip. It permits you to show any two small objects, first in one hand and then the other, and also to show that both hands appear to be otherwise empty, and leaves a duplicate of one of the objects hidden in whichever hand you plan to have it in, depending on the trick you are doing.

Finger-Palm False Count

This is the same thing, done by finger-palming the coins instead of thumb-palming them. To show two coins when you really have three, you might start with an extra one finger-palmed in your right hand. The other two are shown spread out on your left hand, with one of them resting at the base of the two middle fingers in position for finger-palming.

As you turn your left hand over, you finger-palm that coin and keep it, while seeming to drop both coins into your right hand. Then you hold out your right hand to show two coins—the one that was dropped from your left hand and the one that was already in your right hand. That leaves you with the extra coin finger-palmed in your left hand.

Which of the two false-count methods you use is a matter of personal preference. But it is a good idea to learn various ways of accomplishing the same magical results, so you can choose the moves that seem most natural for you in performing a particular trick.

2

DO-ANYWHERE TRICKS WITH COINS AND BILLS

UP ONE SLEEVE AND DOWN THE OTHER

How it looks

"Magicians are always being accused of making things go up their sleeves," you say to the audience, "and that's exactly what I'm going to do." You show a coin, put it into your left hand, and close that hand around it.

Pointing to your left arm with your other hand, you explain, "I'm going to make it go up this sleeve, across my back, down my other sleeve, and then flip over twice so it will land right inside my pocket." You pull out the right-hand pocket of your slacks to show it empty and then push it back in again. "I'll bet you don't believe I can do that, do you? Neither do I. But let's try."

You jerk back your closed left hand as if shooting the coin from that hand up your sleeve, open your hand and show it empty, wiggle your shoulders as if the coin were passing across your back, and shake your right arm as though it were coming down your other sleeve.

"Did you see it flip over twice and land right in my pocket?" you ask. "Well, it did." Showing your right hand empty, you put it into what was the empty pocket and take out the coin. "That always surprises me," you say. "I've never figured out how I do it."

What you need

All you need is a half-dollar or quarter in the otherwise empty right-hand pocket of your slacks.

What you do

Reach into the pocket with your right hand, bring out the coin between your thumb and fingers, hold it up to show it, and let it drop from your fingertips to the palm of that hand. Lower the right hand to display the coin and bounce it flat so it slides to the base of the two middle fingers in position for finger-palming.

Hold out your left hand, fingertips toward the audience and cupped upward slightly. Turn your right hand over toward you and bring it down inside your partly cupped left-hand fingers as if to drop the coin, but keep it finger-palmed in your right hand. As you draw your hands apart, close the left fingers as though holding the coin, and keep that closed left hand held out in front of you.

Without hesitating, immediately touch the tip of your right first finger against your left sleeve as you point to it and say, "I'm going to make it go up this sleeve...." Run the tip of your pointing finger up along the sleeve toward your shoulder.

In a continuing motion, with the finger pointing up toward the ceiling, turn the right hand with its palm toward the audience and move it out away from you and across from left to right, making a sweeping outward half-circle at chest level, as you say, "Across my back...."

UP ONE SLEEVE AND DOWN THE OTHER

Audience views

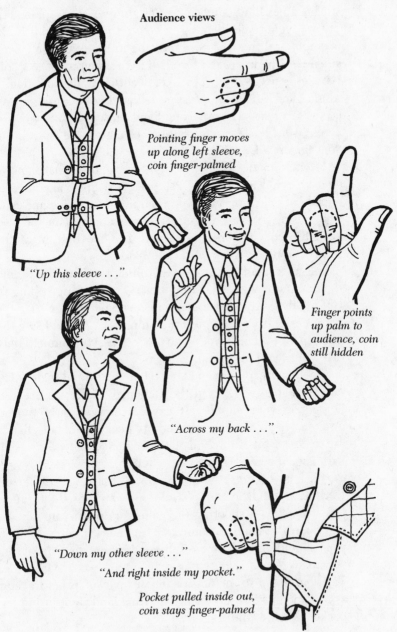

Pointing finger moves up along left sleeve, coin finger-palmed

"Up this sleeve . . ."

Finger points up palm to audience, coin still hidden

"Across my back . . .".

"Down my other sleeve . . ."

"And right inside my pocket."

Pocket pulled inside out, coin stays finger-palmed

37

This gives the audience a brief glimpse of the palm side of your right hand, helping to create the impression that it is empty and that the coin must be in the closed left hand still held out in front of you. But the finger-palmed coin remains concealed by your loosely curled right-hand fingers as the first finger points upward and your hand moves across. You simply turn your hand outward and sweep it across from left to right without changing the position of your fingers. "Down the other sleeve. . . ."

As you look down at your right sleeve, drop that hand to your side and tap the still-extended first finger against the outside of your pocket. "And then flip over twice and land right inside my pocket." Put your hand into the pocket, keep the coin finger-palmed, and grip the bottom of the pocket lining between your thumb and first finger.

Pull your hand out, to pull the lining inside out, and hold the lining out with your thumb and finger still gripping it. Hold it that way long enough for everyone to see that the pocket is empty. Then push the lining back in and leave the finger-palmed coin inside the pocket as you immediately take your hand out again.

All of your explanation about what you intend to do takes only a moment. The coin the audience thinks you are still holding in your closed left hand is now secretly tucked away inside your presumably empty pocket, and both hands are really empty. But as far as the audience knows, the trick hasn't started yet. All the rest is acting.

"I'll bet you don't believe I can do that. . . . Neither do I!" you say. "But let's try." Hold out your closed left hand, jerk it back as if shooting the coin from it up your sleeve, and open the hand to show that the coin is gone. Wiggle your shoulders slightly as if the coin were passing across your back. Then shake your right arm down at your side. Tap your finger to the outside of your pocket as before, and ask, "Did you see it flip over twice and land right inside my pocket? Well, it did."

Hold up your right hand to show it empty and put it into your pocket. Get the coin between your finger and thumb and bring it out to hold it up and show it as you say, "That always surprises me. I've never figured out how I do it."

CASH OFFER

How it looks
You take a facial tissue from your pocket, shake it open to show clearly that there is nothing in it, and roll it into a small ball in your hands. Holding it up, you ask, "If I offered to sell you this for a dime, would you buy it?"

Without waiting for an answer, you snap your fingers over the ball of tissue, tear it open, and remove a shining half-dollar from inside it. As you show the half-dollar, you say, "For a dime, you should have bought it!"

What you need
A standard-size facial tissue
A shiny new half-dollar

How you fix it
Open out the facial tissue, stuff it loosely into the otherwise empty right-hand pocket of your jacket, and put the half-dollar into the pocket with it.

What you do
Reach into your pocket, get the half-dollar finger-palmed in your right hand, grip part of the tissue between your thumb and first finger, and take it from your pocket with your other fingers loosely curled inward to hide the coin.

Bring both hands in front of you, their backs toward the audience, and open out the tissue so as to hold it up by one top corner between your right thumb and first finger and the opposite corner between your left thumb and finger.

CASH OFFER

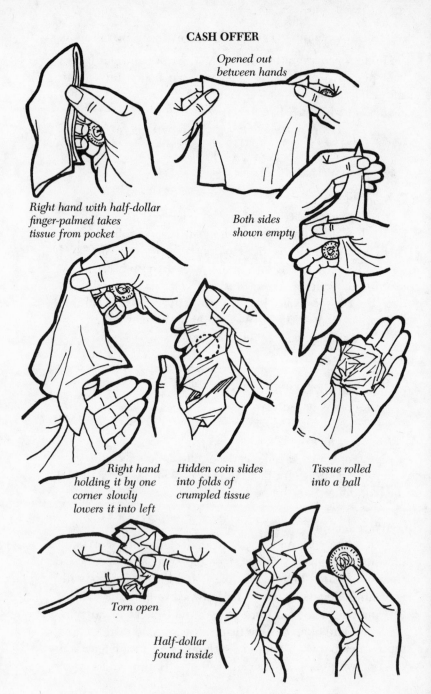

Right hand with half-dollar
finger-palmed takes
tissue from pocket

Opened out
between hands

Both sides
shown empty

Right hand
holding it by one
corner slowly
lowers it into left

Hidden coin slides
into folds of
crumpled tissue

Tissue rolled
into a ball

Torn open

Half-dollar
found inside

Shake it out to show it is empty, move your left hand forward and all the way over to the right to show the other side of the tissue, and bring both hands back as they were with the tissue stretched between them.

Drop the left corner from your left hand so the tissue hangs down from your right hand. Shake it again with your right hand and show your left hand empty. Cup your left hand in front of you, fingers toward the front, and bring your right hand above it so the botton corner of the tissue touches the left palm.

Slowly lower your right hand so the tissue loosely folds itself down into your cupped left hand. As your hands touch together, with your right hand inside the folds of the partly crumpled tissue, let the finger-palmed coin slide into it. Keeping your hands together, fold the tissue up around the coin and quickly roll it into a ball. Hold it on your left palm, with that thumb resting lightly on top of it to keep it from unrolling, and take your right hand away.

Display the ball of tissue on your outstretched left palm and ask, "If I offered to sell you this for a dime, would you buy it?" Show your right hand empty and snap your fingers over the tissue. Take it with both hands, slowly tear it open, and bring the half-dollar into view. Throw the tissue aside, hold up the half-dollar, and say, "For a dime, you should have bought it!"

BREAKING A HALF INTO QUARTERS

How it looks
"There are people who claim the strange psychic ability to bend keys and spoons and other things made of solid metal with the power of the mind," you say with mock seriousness as you begin this magical spoof. "I can't do that, but sometimes I can break a half-dollar in half."

You take a half-dollar from your pocket, hold it at the fingertips of your upright left hand, and start squeezing it with your right hand, as you explain with a smile, "I don't use mind power . . . just brute strength."

As you lift your right hand away, you ask, "And what do you get when you break a half in half?" Fanned out at your left fingertips, in place of the half-dollar that was there, you show two 25-cent pieces. You drop them singly from your left fingertips into your right hand and say, "Why, two quarters, of course."

What you need

A half-dollar and two quarters, which you have in an empty right-hand pocket at the start

What you do

Reach into your pocket, stack the two quarters, and push them up into the crotch of your right thumb to hold them thumb-palmed together. Get the half-dollar clipped by its sides between your first two fingers and bring it out to show it with the back of your hand toward the spectators. (Your remarks about the psychic power to bend keys and spoons will give you time to position the coins in your hand inside your pocket without rushing it, as if you were searching among the change in your pocket to find the half-dollar.)

Hold your left hand outstretched, drop the half-dollar into it from your right hand, and let your right hand fall to your side. Display the coin on your left palm and tilt your hand so as to slide it forward. Hold it by its edge between your thumb and fingertips as you raise your hand into position for the fingertip drop, with the back of the hand toward the spectators, fingers pointing upward, and the half-dollar visible from in front at your fingertips.

As you say, "I don't use mind power . . . just brute strength," bring your right hand up, fingertips toward the left, so it goes horizontally across in front of your upright left fingers, screening the half-dollar from front view. Let the half-dollar secretly drop from your left fingertips and slide down into that hand in finger-palm position. With

BREAKING A HALF INTO QUARTERS

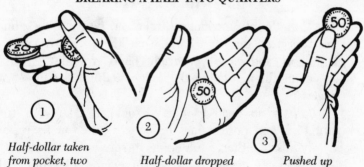

① Half-dollar taken
from pocket, two
quarters thumb-palmed

② Half-dollar dropped
into left hand

③ Pushed up
to fingertips

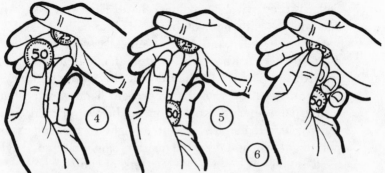

④ Right hand comes
to squeeze half-dollar

⑤ It slides down
into left hand
and is finger-palmed

⑥ Left thumb
and fingers take
the two quarters

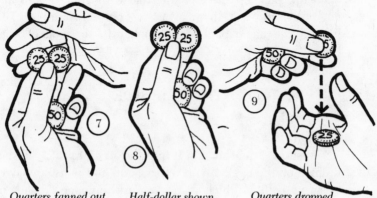

⑦ Quarters fanned out
at left fingertips

⑧ Half-dollar shown
"broken" into quarters

⑨ Quarters dropped
singly into
empty right hand

your left thumb and fingers, take the two thumb-palmed quarters from the right hand. Slide them slightly apart to fan them, and close your right hand around them as if squeezing the half-dollar the audience thinks is still at your fingertips.

There is no need to hurry. You can take your time switching and positioning the coins while you keep your two hands together, pretending to squeeze and break the half-dollar. If necessary, you can even push your right thumb down inside your left hand to make sure the half-dollar is properly finger-palmed there. Then you ask, "And what do you get when you break a half in half?"

Keep your left hand as it is and take your right hand away to reveal the two quarters fanned at your left fingertips in place of the half-dollar. Hold them that way a moment. Let it be seen that your right hand is empty and turn it palm upward about six inches below your left hand. Turn your left hand over, left to right so the fingers are pointing down, and drop the quarters singly into your right hand as you say, "Why, two quarters, of course."

Let your left hand fall to your side and jingle the quarters on your right palm to show them. Finally bring your left hand up, pick up the two quarters with your thumb and fingertips, and put them away in your left-hand pocket, leaving the finger-palmed half-dollar in the pocket with them.

THE FLIP SIDE

How it looks

You show a quarter, flip it into the air, catch it, and slap it down on the back of your other hand, in the usual way of tossing a coin. "Which is it," you ask someone, "heads or tails?" Whatever his guess, you lift your fingers, show him the coin, and pick it up as you say, "Let's try again."

But as you seem to flip it into the air a second time, the

THE FLIP SIDE

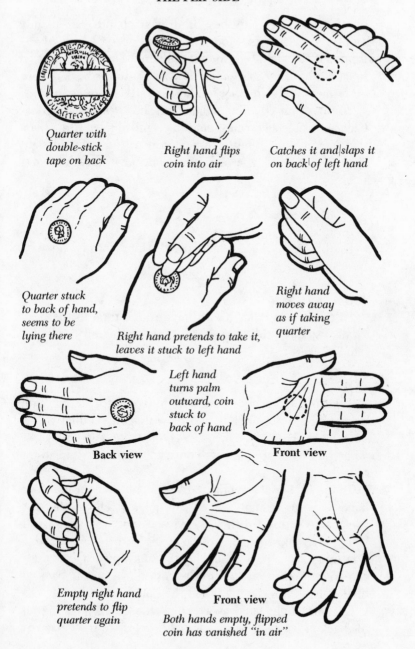

Quarter with double-stick tape on back

Right hand flips coin into air

Catches it and slaps it on back of left hand

Quarter stuck to back of hand, seems to be lying there

Right hand pretends to take it, leaves it stuck to left hand

Right hand moves away as if taking quarter

Left hand turns palm outward, coin stuck to back of hand

Back view

Front view

Empty right hand pretends to flip quarter again

Front view

Both hands empty, flipped coin has vanished "in air"

45

quarter suddenly vanishes. Both your hands are plainly empty, your fingers wide apart. "I'm sorry," you say. "I flipped it too high. But there it is again." You reach out as if to catch the "invisible" coin, then slap it to the back of your other hand and announce, "This time, it's heads."

You lift your covering fingers and show that the coin has become visible again and that it has landed heads up, as you said it would. "I'd better quit before it fades out of sight again," you say as you pick it up and put it back into your pocket.

What you need

A quarter

Double-stick transparent tape, the kind that is sticky on both sides

How you fix it

Fasten a ¾-inch length of double-stick tape to the back ("tails" side) of the quarter and have the coin in a right-hand pocket.

What you do

Take out the quarter, show it, flip it into the air with your right thumb, catch it, and show it again on the palm of your hand. Flip it once more, catch it, and loosely close your right hand around it as you ask, "Which is it, heads or tails?"

That gives you a moment to feel the coin inside your hand with your thumb, so you can quickly tell whether the sticky side is upward. If it is, leave it that way; if not, tilt your partly closed hand so the quarter turns over, sticky side up. Hold out your left hand, back upward, and turn your right hand over to slap the coin down on the back of the left hand, pressing down so the quarter sticks to it.

Lift your right hand away, show the quarter resting on the back of your left hand, and hold it close to the person as you point to it and either congratulate him for guessing correctly or tell him that he missed. Whatever his guess, you say, "Let's try again."

Move your left hand back a little and turn your body slightly to the left. Cover the coin with your right fingers just as if you were picking it up with those fingers and thumb. Sweep your fingers lightly across it, as if taking it, and at the same time turn your left hand palm outward, with its fingers spread widely apart. The quarter is now stuck to the back of your left hand, with the empty palm of that hand toward the spectator so it appears that you must have taken the coin with your right hand.

Without hesitating, continue to bring your right hand to the right as though it had the coin. Go through the motions of pretending to flip it into the air with your thumb. Look upward as though watching the coin. Open your right hand wide, fingers spread apart so it can be seen that both hands are empty, and say, "I'm sorry. I flipped it too high." Reach out with your right hand as though to catch it from the air. "But there it is again."

Immediately slap your right hand to the top of your left hand. Announce, "This time, it's heads." As your right fingers cover your left hand, turn your left hand palm downward, which brings the coin under your right fingers. Lift your right hand away and show the quarter visibly resting on the back of your left hand again. Hold it close to the spectator and point to it so that he can see it is "heads up" as you said it would be. Then pick it up from the back of your left hand and put it away in your pocket.

(Note: The tape must be really sticky to hold the quarter to the back of your hand, so replace it after you have used it a few times. Just peel the old strip off with your thumbnail and apply a fresh one.)

FOLDING THE DOLLAR BILL

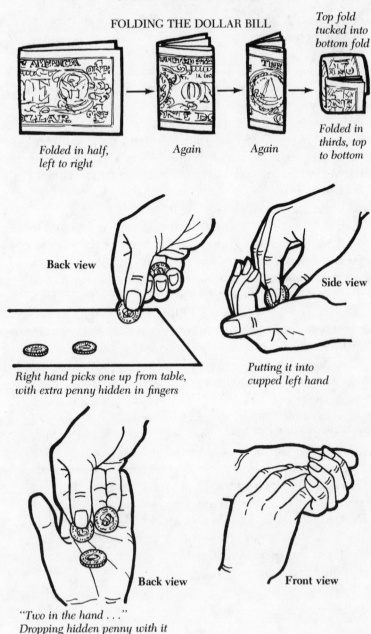

Top fold tucked into bottom fold

Folded in half, left to right

Again

Again

Folded in thirds, top to bottom

Back view

Side view

Right hand picks one up from table, with extra penny hidden in fingers

Putting it into cupped left hand

Back view

Front view

"Two in the hand ..."
Dropping hidden penny with it

ONE HUNDRED AND TWO

How it looks

"This is a little test of your powers of observation," you say as you take three pennies from your pocket and put them out on a table. Picking them up one at a time, you put two of them into your other hand and the third one into your pocket. "How many are in my hand?" you ask. The answer will be two, but you open your hand to show that all three pennies are in it.

You repeat the same thing, singly putting two into your hand and the third into your pocket, and again open your hand and drop out three. "I'll do it one last time," you say. "One cent in my hand . . . two cents in my hand . . . and the third one goes into my pocket. How many are in my hand?"

Whatever the answer, you say, "I'm sorry. You weren't watching closely. I have in my hand . . . exactly one hundred and two." You turn your hand over and drop out two. "One cent . . . two cents." Then you reach into your hand and produce a one-dollar bill as you say, "And that's exactly one hundred more."

What you need

A dollar bill

Four pennies, either all new or all old, so they look somewhat alike

How you fix it

Put the dollar bill on a table so its long edges are at the top and bottom. Fold it in half from left to right, in half the same way again, and then once more. Now fold the top third down, vertically from top to center, and the bottom third up, from bottom to center. Finally, tuck the top fold inside the bottom fold and crease the folds so it all stays together in a compact little package. Folded that way, the bill is not much bigger than a penny.

Have the folded bill and four pennies in the right-hand pocket of your jacket.

What you do

Reach into your pocket with your right hand. Gather up the pennies, making sure you have all four, and close your fingers loosely around them. Bring your hand out and hold it a little above the top of the table. With your thumb, push off three of the pennies, one at a time, dropping them on the table. Leave the fourth one in your hand, hidden by your partly closed fingers. There is no need to palm it; just keep your three lower fingers closed enough to hold it.

Hold your left hand palm upward, fingers toward the front. Pick up one of the coins from the table with your right thumb and first finger and put it into your left hand, closing it as you say, "One cent in my hand."

Pick up another with your right hand and open your cupped left hand enough so your right hand can go down into it. As you leave the second penny, let the hidden one secretly drop from your right hand with it, so the two go together into your left hand. There are now three in your hand, but you say, "Two cents in my hand."

Pick up the last penny from the table with your right hand and say, "And the third one goes into my pocket." Show it and put your hand into your pocket as if to leave it there. But just keep it hidden in your fingers instead of leaving it in your pocket and immediately bring your hand out again and let it fall to your side for a moment.

Ask, "How many are in my hand?" The spectators should say there are two. Turn your left hand over, drop the three pennies from it to the table, one at a time, and then turn that hand palm upward and say, "I'll do it again."

Pick up one from the table with your right hand and put it into your left. "One in my hand." Pick up another and put that into your cupped left hand, letting the penny in your right hand secretly drop with it. "Two in my hand." Pick up the third one and say, as before, "And the third one goes into my pocket."

Show it and put your hand into your pocket. But this time, really drop the penny into your pocket, leave it there, and scoop up the folded dollar bill so it is hidden in your fingers. Immediately bring your hand out again and let it fall to your side. Just keep your fingers loosely closed around the folded bill, the same way as you hid the penny before.

Once more ask, "How many in my hand?" Some spectators may say there are two and some may say three. Whatever the answer, open your left hand and drop out the three pennies. Say, "I'll do it one last time."

Pick up one penny and put it into your left hand. "One cent in my hand." Pick up the second and put that into the left hand, secretly leaving the dollar bill with it. "Two cents in my hand." Pick up the last penny, show it, put it into your pocket, and leave it there as you say, "And the third one goes into my pocket. . . . How many are in my hand?"

Finally say, "I have in my hand exactly one hundred and two." Turn your left hand over, fingers downward and count out two pennies on the table, but still keep that hand partly closed. "One cent . . . two cents." Show your right hand empty, reach up into your left hand, and with the help of both hands quickly open out the dollar bill to show it as you say, "And that's exactly one hundred more."

THE STRAPHANGER

How it looks

You take a nickel from your pocket, hold it at your fingertips, and transfer it from hand to hand, showing your hands otherwise empty. A touch of your fingers instantly changes the nickel to a half-dollar, and you again show your hands empty before you put it away in your pocket.

THE STRAPHANGER

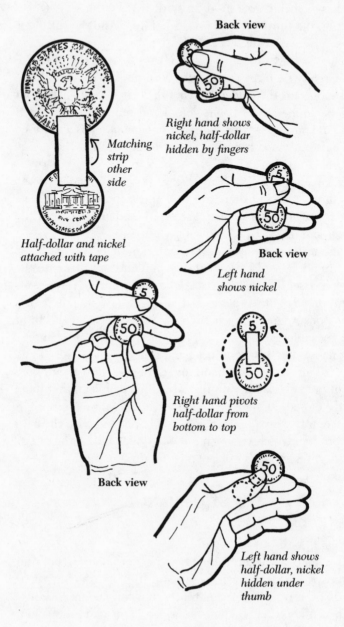

Matching strip other side

Half-dollar and nickel attached with tape

Back view

Right hand shows nickel, half-dollar hidden by fingers

Left hand shows nickel

Back view

Right hand pivots half-dollar from bottom to top

Back view

Left hand shows half-dollar, nickel hidden under thumb

52

What you need
A nickel
A half-dollar
Transparent tape

How you fix it
The instant change from nickel to half-dollar is accomplished with a simply made trick coin. Put the half-dollar on a table and the nickel ½ inch below it. Leaving that space between them, fasten a strip of transparent tape from one to the other. Turn over the attached coins and fasten a matching strip of tape at the back, sticking the tapes together where they meet between the coins. The result is that if you hold up one coin, the other will hang directly beneath it at the end of the attached tape.

Have the trick coin in an empty right-hand pocket.

What you do
Reach into the pocket with your right hand and take the nickel between your thumb and first finger so the tips of them hold the very edge of it and the attached half-dollar lies inside your fingers. Bring your hand out with the back of it toward the audience, fingers pointed toward the left, and hold up the nickel to show it. The half-dollar hangs behind your fingers, which hide it from front view.

Show your left hand empty and then take the nickel with that hand by bringing your left fingers over in front of the right fingers, backs of both hands toward the audience, and gripping the bottom edge of the nickel between your left thumb and first finger. Draw your right hand down and away from your left. This leaves the nickel displayed by your left hand as it previously was by your right hand. The half-dollar hangs hidden behind your left fingers.

The sudden change is now made by one quick continuous movement of the right hand, with the left thumb acting as a pivot. The left thumb doesn't move; it rests as it is, lightly against the tape between the two coins. Just bring your right hand up from beneath into the palm of the left hand, grip the hanging half-dollar with your right thumb and fingers, and swing it out to the right and on up to the top.

This swings the whole tape around from bottom to top in a counterclockwise circular motion, like a spindle on a dial, bringing the half-dollar up to where your thumb can hold it, and at the same time bringing the nickel down under your left thumb.

Immediately take your right hand away, show it empty, and display the half-dollar at your left fingertips in place of the nickel that was there. Shake your left hand a little to wiggle the half-dollar at your fingertips so viewers are fully aware of the sudden change. Press your left thumb against the tape and hidden nickel and turn your left hand outward to the left, palm toward the audience, to show both sides of the half-dollar. Then put it away in a left-hand pocket and leave it there.

MONEY IN MIND

How it looks

"I'd like to try a little experiment in mind control," you say. "I know I have no power to control your minds, so I'm going to ask one of you to try to control *my* mind." You choose one of the persons watching. "You impress me as someone with a strong mind. Just for fun, would you like to try it?"

You take a handful of change from your pocket, pick out a quarter, a nickel, a penny, and a dime, and put the four coins on a table. "I want you to think of any one of those four coins," you say. "Don't tell me which one. But once you have decided, please don't change your mind. Just keep thinking about that one coin."

From your pocket, you remove four little manila envelopes. You drop one coin into each envelope, close the

MONEY IN MIND

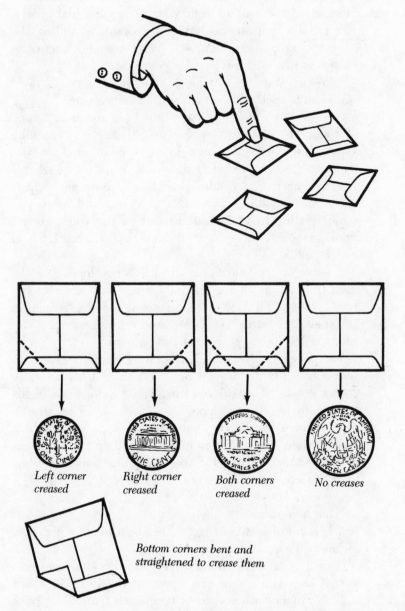

Left corner
creased

Right corner
creased

Both corners
creased

No creases

Bottom corners bent and
straightened to crease them

flaps, and spread the envelopes face down on the table. "Please mix these all up so they are in no particular order," you tell the person, as you demonstrate by sliding the envelopes around on the table. "Mix them so neither of us can guess which coin is in what envelope."

You turn your head while that is being done. "Now I want you to spell out the name of the coin you are thinking about, one letter at a time, each time I tap my finger on one of these envelopes," you explain. "Don't say anything aloud. Just spell the name in your own mind. If you happened to be thinking of the dime, for instance, when I tap my finger, you would spell 'D.' Then when I tap it again, you would spell 'I' . . . and so on. And when you finish spelling to yourself the name of the coin you are thinking about, just put your hand over mine. Do you understand?"

Slowly you tap your finger to various envelopes, pausing each time as the person mentally spells one letter of the coin in mind. "I'll try to get an impression of the thought as you spell each letter," you say. "And remember, when you spell the last letter, put your hand on mine."

The person finishes the silent spelling and puts a hand on yours. You ask him to call out the name of his mentally chosen coin. "Now will you open the envelope our hands happen to be resting upon," you say. "Let's see if the experiment worked." He opens the envelope and inside it finds the one coin he had in mind. "You didn't know it was there and neither did I," you say, "but somehow your thoughts led me to it."

What you need

A handful of small change, including a dime, a penny, a nickel, and a quarter

Four 2 × 2 inch manila envelopes, the kind coin collectors use, with a flap that opens at the top. These are available in most variety stores at counters that sell supplies for collectors.

How you fix it

The secret depends in part on the fact that when the coins are considered in order according to their size, the name of each coin has one more letter than the coin before it: *dime* has four letters, *penny*, five letters, *nickel*, six, and *quarter*, seven. Actually, you don't know until the very end of the trick which coin the person has in mind, but because of the successive spelling the last one you touch is always the mentally chosen one.

That much of the trick works automatically, as will be explained, and is nothing you have to think about while performing it. But since the coins are inside envelopes and you can't see them to tell which ones to touch in order, the envelopes must be secretly "marked" so that you know where each coin is after the envelopes have been mixed up on the table. They are "marked" by creasing the bottom corners.

Hold one of the envelopes so its flap end is at the top. At the *bottom* of that envelope, fold up the tip of the *left* corner and crease it firmly, then fold the same corner to the back, crease it again, and finally straighten it out, leaving the crease mark. In the same way, crease the *right* bottom corner of a second envelope. Crease *both* bottom corners, left and right, of a third envelope. Leave the fourth envelope plain and *uncreased*.

Make sure the corner crease marks are clearly visible, so you can identify each envelope at a glance. These crease marks may seem obvious to you, because you know where to look for them, but to the spectators they will appear to be creases made accidentally while carrying the envelopes around in your pocket and handling them. Even if they were noticed, which isn't likely, the mental spelling out of the name of the coin, which leads your finger right to it, would remain a puzzle.

The coins are *always* put into the envelopes according to size order, from small to large. The dime goes into the envelope with its left corner creased, the penny into the one with its right corner creased, the nickel into the envelope with both corners creased, and the quarter into the uncreased envelope. When the coins are in their proper envelopes, all you have to remember is: left, right, both, none.

Have the coins in the pocket in which you usually carry your change and the four empty envelopes, in any order, in one of your other pockets.

What you do

Take out the handful of change, pick out the four coins, and spread them across the table in any order. Ask the person to think of any one of the coins, but not to say which one. Take out the little envelopes and drop those on the table.

Pick up any envelope, glance at its corners, and then pick up the coin that belongs in that envelope. (If you happened to pick up the envelope with its right corner creased, for instance, you would know the penny belonged in that one.) Drop it into the envelope, close the flap, and put it flap upward on the table. Continue until all four coins are in their proper envelopes.

Explain to the person that you want the envelopes mixed up, and demonstrate by sliding them around on the table to mix them. Then turn your head away while the person mixes them, "so that neither of us can guess which coin is in what envelope."

Now it is necessary to give very clear instructions about the mental spelling out of the name of the coin the person has in mind. Follow the patter as given, explaining that one letter is to be spelled silently each time you tap your finger, and that when the spelling is finished the person is to put his hand over yours. This is important so that he will stop you when he has finished mentally spelling out his chosen coin. After you start the tapping, remind him again by saying, "And remember, when you spell the last letter, put your hand on mine."

Tap your finger on any envelope and wait a moment, as if you were trying to get a "mental impression" of the first letter the person silently spelled. Then tap any other, wait, and then tap a third one. The first three times, it makes no difference what envelopes you tap. But starting with the fourth one, you must tap each in order, wherever that particular envelope happens to be on the table.

Forget about the coins inside the envelopes. Just think: left, right, both, none. When you come to the fourth tap, simply look for the envelope with its left corner creased. Put your finger on that and wait a moment. If the person mentally chose the dime, he will put his hand on yours (because it takes four letters, four taps, to spell out the word *dime.*) If he doesn't stop you, then look for the envelope with its right corner creased and tap your finger on that. Again, wait a second; if he doesn't stop you, next tap the one with both corners creased. Finally, if you are still not stopped, tap the one with no corners creased.

With the envelopes mixed up on the table the flaps may be in various positions, not always directly facing you at the top. Always glance first at the flap, then at the creased corners in relation to the way the flap may be turned. The presentation allows you plenty of time between each tap of your finger to make sure which envelope should be next.

When the person puts his hand on yours, ask him to call out the name of the coin he had in mind. Have him open the envelope and show the coin to everybody, and say, "You didn't know it was there and neither did I, but somehow your thoughts led me to it."

ONE AND ONE MAKE THREE

How it looks

"The hand is never quicker than the eye," you say as you take a dollar bill from your pocket, unfold it, and show both sides of it. "Scientists will tell you that old saying about the

ONE AND ONE MAKE THREE

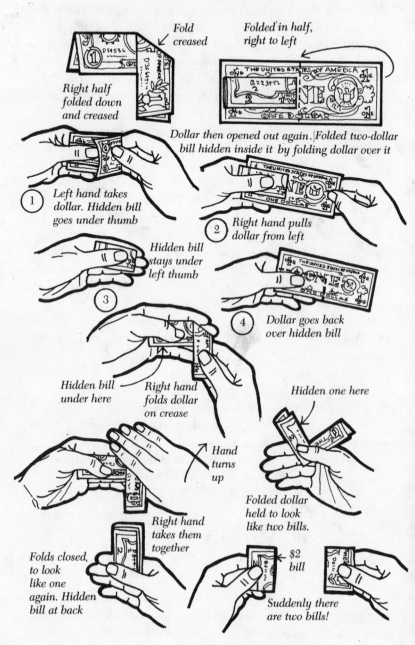

Fold creased

Folded in half, right to left

Right half folded down and creased

Dollar then opened out again. Folded two-dollar bill hidden inside it by folding dollar over it

1. Left hand takes dollar. Hidden bill goes under thumb

2. Right hand pulls dollar from left

3. Hidden bill stays under left thumb

4. Dollar goes back over hidden bill

Hidden bill under here

Right hand folds dollar on crease

Hidden one here

Hand turns up

Folded dollar held to look like two bills.

Right hand takes them together

Folds closed, to look like one again. Hidden bill at back

$2 bill

Suddenly there are two bills!

swiftness of the hand just isn't true. But sometimes the eyes can be fooled by a very simple optical illusion that makes people think the hand is quicker. If I fold this dollar bill so the two ends are held out separately . . . it looks like two dollars instead of just one, doesn't it?"

You fold the bill and hold it so that the two separate ends sticking up out of your hand look like two bills, and carefully show that your hands are otherwise empty. "If I had it secretly folded like that and just showed it to you that way, you might believe I had two," you say. You straighten the two ends so they are together. "I mean, if you didn't know I had only one."

Suddenly you draw your hands apart and there *are* two folded bills, one in each hand. "Of course, it's only an optical illusion." You unfold one of the bills and drop it open on the table. "Because I really have three dollars . . . not two." You point to the one on the table. "That's one. . . ." Quickly you unfold the other one and show that it is a two-dollar bill, and drop that on top of the first one as you joke, "And here's *two*."

What you need
A one-dollar bill
A two-dollar bill

How you fix it
Place the one-dollar bill back upward on a table, long edges top and bottom, and fold it in half, top to bottom. Now fold the right half over and down toward you, folding it upon the bill diagonally at the center to bring that end down until it points directly toward the rear edge of the table. The right half should now be vertical, the left half horizontal. Crease the diagonal fold with your thumbnail. Then open out the bill again.

Put the two-dollar bill back upward on the table, long edges top and bottom, and fold it in half, top to bottom.

Fold it in half again from right to left, and crease the folds so it will lie flat. Place the folded two-dollar bill, with its open edges toward the left, on the left side of the one-dollar bill.

Fold the one-dollar bill in half from right to left so the folded two-dollar bill is hidden inside it. Turn them so the center fold of the outer bill is toward the bottom, and have them that way in the otherwise empty left-hand pocket of your slacks.

What you do

As you talk about the quickness of the hand and simple optical illusions that can fool the eye, take out the folded bill, hold it pressed together, and show both sides of it. Transfer it to your right hand, which takes the center folded edge between thumb and fingers. Casually show your left hand empty and then bring that hand in front of you, palm cupped toward you, back of the hand toward the audience.

Bring your right hand over to return the bill to your left hand, open edges of the bill toward the left. As you take it with your left hand, push your left thumb inside the bill, under the top fold, so the two-dollar bill concealed within it comes into the crotch of the thumb and the thumb lies across it. Pushing your thumb into the outer bill partly opens its top fold. With your right hand, take that right edge of the outer bill and open it out all the way.

This should look as though you merely put the folded bill into your left hand to hold it and pushed it partly open with your left thumb so your right hand could unfold it. At this point, the left edges of the folded two-dollar bill are in the crotch of your left thumb, which lies across it behind the opened dollar bill. The dollar bill is stretched between your hands, with your right thumb and fingers holding the right edge of it.

Press your left thumb on the concealed two-dollar bill. With your right hand, pull the dollar bill away from your left hand, keeping the hidden bill under your left thumb. Shake open the dollar bill with your right hand to show it. Then put it back into your left hand so the edge slides back under your left thumb, on top of the hidden bill. The lower-left part of the open dollar bill should now be exactly on top of the folded two-dollar bill, with your left thumb holding both.

Turn your left hand out to the left, palm outward, to show the open dollar, which covers the hidden bill, and then bring your left palm toward you again. With your right hand, fold the dollar in half from top to bottom against your left palm. Then fold the right half of it over and down toward you, folding it diagonally at the center. (This is the way you first folded it on the table when you were preparing the bill for the trick, so it is already well creased and will fold easily.)

The horizontal left half of the diagonally folded bill now lies directly over the folded two-dollar bill. Square them together at the left and bottom edges with your right hand as it finishes folding the dollar bill. From now on, keep them exactly together.

Turn your right hand palm downward and bring your right thumb *under* the folded center of both bills, so that your right first finger lies across the top corner of the diagonal fold. Hold that corner tightly between your right thumb and fingers and then turn your right hand up so the back of it is toward the audience.

The two folded halves of the dollar bill now stick up above the top of your right hand, separated so that from the front they look somewhat like two bills. Say, "If I fold this dollar so the two ends are held out separately, it looks like two dollars instead of just one, doesn't it?" The two-dollar bill remains hidden behind the upright left half of the dollar, squared evenly with it and folded the same way so the whole thing looks like one of the folds of the dollar. Keep them as they are in your right hand and show your left hand empty as you say, "If I had it secretly folded like that and just showed it to you that way, you might believe I had two."

Bring your left hand, palm toward you, in front of your right hand. Close the right fold of the displayed dollar toward the left so that the two separate folds are brought together, as if closing a fan. Lift your left hand away and show what appears to be the single folded dollar sticking up from your right hand, and say, "I mean, if you didn't know I had only one."

Again bring your empty left hand over in front of your right hand. Grip the folded two-dollar bill between your left thumb and fingers, and suddenly pull your hands wide apart, holding a folded bill in each hand, to show there are really two instead of one.

Open out the bill in your right hand with the fingers of that hand, show it, and drop it on the table as you say, "Of course, it's only an optical illusion. . . . Because I really have three dollars, not two." Point to the dollar bill on the table. "That's one. . . ." Quickly unfold the two-dollar bill with your left hand, show it fully opened, and drop it on top of the first one. "And here's *two*."

WINNER TAKE ALL

How it looks

You take an envelope from your pocket, remove a poker chip and a quarter from it, and drop the empty envelope on the table. You pick up the poker chip and put it into the envelope, then pick up the quarter and put that into your pocket. "What's in the envelope?" you ask someone who is watching. He answers that the poker chip is in the envelope. "So far, you're absolutely right," you say. "I'll bet you've played this game before. Let's try it again."

Once more, you put the poker chip into the envelope and

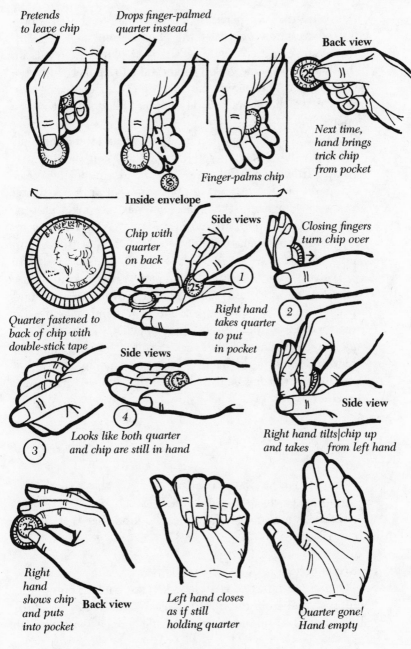

Pretends to leave chip

Drops finger-palmed quarter instead

Back view

Finger-palms chip

Next time, hand brings trick chip from pocket

Inside envelope

Quarter fastened to back of chip with double-stick tape

Chip with quarter on back

Side views

1

Right hand takes quarter to put in pocket

Closing fingers turn chip over

2

Side views

4

Looks like both quarter and chip are still in hand

3

Right hand tilts|chip up and takes | from left hand

Side view

Right hand shows chip and puts into pocket

Back view

Left hand closes as if still holding quarter

Quarter gone! Hand empty

the coin into your pocket and ask what's in the envelope, but when he answers that the chip is, you say, "No, this time you've missed. They've changed places." You dump the quarter from the envelope and take the poker chip from your pocket. "I think it's the envelope that's confusing you. Let's make the game a little simpler. I'll do it out in the open."

You lay the poker chip and the quarter on the outstretched palm of your left hand. Then you pick up the quarter from your hand, close that hand around the poker chip, and put the quarter into your pocket. You ask which one is in your hand. When he says that the poker chip is, you say, "No, I'm afraid you missed again. They're *both* in my hand." You open your left hand and show both the chip and the quarter.

"Maybe it will be easier if I do it the other way around," you say, as you close your left hand over the chip and quarter. You take the chip from your hand, leaving the quarter, and put the chip into your pocket. "Now what's in my hand?" He answers that the quarter is, but you say, "No, there's nothing in my hand." You open your hand to show that the quarter has vanished, and brush your empty hands together as you say, "That's how the game is won. Winner take all."

What you need
An envelope
Three quarters that look alike
Two poker chips that look alike
Double-stick transparent tape, the kind that is sticky on both sides

How you fix it
One of the quarters is attached to the back of one of the chips, so that from the front it looks like only a poker chip, but when it is turned over and lying flat on your hand it

looks like a chip with a quarter on top of it. The quarter is fastened to the chip off-center, so the edge of the coin is close to the edge of the chip, which looks more natural than if it were right at the center.

Put one of the chips on a table. Take a strip of double-stick tape and cut it to a ¾-inch length. Fasten that strip vertically to the chip, starting just below the chip's top edge. Run another strip the same length horizontally across the middle of the first one. Then attach two cross-strips the same length to the back of the quarter. Stick the tapes on the quarter to the tapes on the chip and press the two together firmly with your thumb. (You can glue the quarter to the chip, if you prefer, but if they are taped as explained they will hold together tight with no edges of tape showing.)

Inside the right-hand pocket of most men's jackets there is a little "ticket pocket." Women can have one sewn into blazer or suit jacket pockets. Put the tricked chip in that, so the side with the attached quarter is toward your body. Put one of the other quarters into the bottom of that jacket pocket. Put the remaining chip and quarter into the envelope, close the flap, fold the envelope in half, and have that in the same pocket.

What you do

Take the envelope from your pocket, open it, and slide the chip and quarter out of it onto the table. Show the envelope empty and drop that on the table. "This is a little game with a poker chip and a quarter," you say, as you turn over each of them to show both sides and also to let it be seen that your hands are empty.

With your left hand, pick up the envelope to hold it at the top by its open flap, with the back of the envelope toward you. Take the poker chip with your right hand and put it into the envelope, then pick up the quarter and put that into your right-hand jacket pocket.

Ask what is in the envelope, and when the person answers that the chip is, say, "So far, you're absolutely right." Slide the chip out of the envelope onto the table and put down the envelope. Say, "And, of course, the quarter is in my pocket." Reach into your pocket with your right hand, get one of the quarters finger-palmed, and take the other quarter between your thumb and first finger to bring it out and show it. Then put that quarter on the table next to the chip as you say, "I'll bet you've played this game before. Let's try again."

Pick up the envelope with your left hand to hold it as before. With your right hand, pick up the chip and put your hand into the envelope. Drop the hidden quarter from your fingers into the envelope and with your thumb slide the chip up into your fingers and finger-palm it. Take your hand out of the envelope as though you have left the chip there. Pick up the quarter from the table, show it, put it into your pocket, and leave both the quarter and finger-palmed chip in your pocket as you bring your hand out again.

Ask what's in the envelope and when the answer is that the chip is there, say, "No, this time you've missed. They've changed places." Tip the quarter out of the envelope and put the envelope aside. With your right hand, reach into your pocket and take the chip with the attached quarter from the little "ticket pocket." Keep the back of it toward you as you bring it out and hold it up to show it as though it were the same chip you had been using before.

"I think it's the envelope that's confusing you," you say. "Let's make the game a little simpler. I'll do it out in the open." Hold your left hand outstretched, palm upward, fingertips toward the front. Lay the poker chip on the fingers of that hand with the quarter side down. Then pick up the quarter from the table and lay that on your left palm in back of the chip. Show them both on your outstretched left hand.

Take away the quarter with your right hand and close

your left hand in a loose fist around the chip, closing the fingertips back against the palm. That automatically turns the chip over inside your left hand, so the side with the attached quarter is now facing upward in the closed hand. Keep the left hand closed. With your right hand, openly put the quarter into your pocket and leave it there, bringing your hand out to show it empty.

Ask whether the quarter or poker chip is in your left hand. When the person answers that the chip is, you say, "No, I'm afraid you missed again. They're *both* in my hand." Open your left hand and show the chip with the attached quarter lying on top of it.

"Maybe it will be easier if I do it the other way around," you say. Keep your left hand outstretched as it is and close the fingers of that hand loosely around the chip and attached quarter. Bring your right thumb and first finger to the side of the left hand, opening that hand enough so that they can go inside and grip the edge of the chip, but keep the left fingertips cupped upward at the front. Hold the *very edge* of the chip between your right thumb and finger, tilt the chip up so the attached quarter is hidden at the back, and take it from your left hand.

Keep your left hand closed as though it still held a quarter. Show the chip with your right hand, spreading your fingers open wide so everyone can see that you have nothing else in that hand, and put the chip into your pocket. Leave it there and bring your right hand out.

Move your closed left hand forward a little and ask, "Now what's in my hand?" When the person answers that you are holding the quarter, say, "No, there's nothing in my hand." Open your left hand slowly, show that the quarter has vanished, and brush both hands together as you say, "That's how the game is won. Winner take all."

3

NOVEL MONEY MAGIC

TOPSY-TURVY

How it looks

"I'll show you how to train a dollar to do tricks for you," you say, as you take a dollar bill from your pocket, unfold it, and hold it between your hands, so the audience can see the full face of the bill. "If you fold it in half from left to right, then fold it again, and open it up . . . it will stand on its head for you—upside down."

You show that the design on the face of the bill has turned upside down. "But if you fold it in half from right to left, fold it again, and open it up . . . it's back on its feet—right side up," you say, as you do that and show that the design has righted itself again.

"Some of you probably know that little trick," you say, as you pretend to explain. "If you turn it from right to left, it stays head up." Without folding the bill at all, you turn it

70

TOPSY-TURVY

MAKING THE TOPSY-TURVY BILL

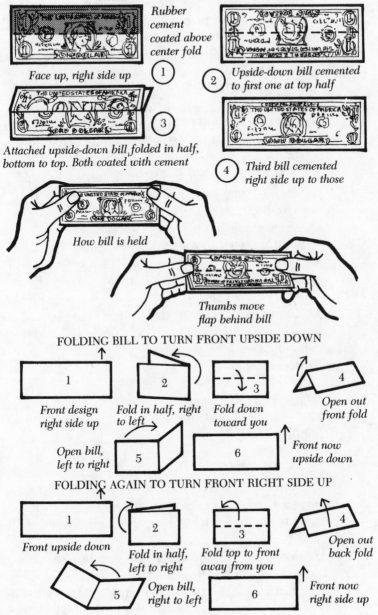

Rubber cement coated above center fold

1 Face up, right side up

2 Upside-down bill cemented to first one at top half

3 Attached upside-down bill folded in half, bottom to top. Both coated with cement

4 Third bill cemented right side up to those

How bill is held

Thumbs move flap behind bill

FOLDING BILL TO TURN FRONT UPSIDE DOWN

1 Front design right side up

2 Fold in half, right to left

3 Fold down toward you

4 Open out front fold

5 Open bill, left to right

6 Front now upside down

FOLDING AGAIN TO TURN FRONT RIGHT SIDE UP

1 Front upside down

2 Fold in half, left to right

3 Fold top to front away from you

4 Open out back fold

5 Open bill, right to left

6 Front now right side up

from front to back a few times, showing both sides right side up. "But if you turn it from left to right, then it flips itself over—upside down." Still without folding it, you turn it again. The full back of it is now right side up, but the face of it is upside down.

You repeat that, pretending to explain once more, and again the designs on the front and back turn topsy-turvy. As you turn the whole bill from front to back in one direction, both sides are normally right side up. But as you turn it in the other direction, the back is right side up and the face upside down. "Just don't turn it from top to bottom," you say, "because that gets very confusing." You do that and now there is a face design on *both* sides of the bill, but no back design at all.

"Turn it from left to right," you say, doing that, "and it's upside down." You show that it is. "But just turn it from right to left and we're back where we started—heads up again." You show both sides of the bill are now normal and right side up once more. "If that's all clear to you. . . I hope somebody will explain it to me," you say as you fold the bill and put it back into your pocket. "Because I just don't understand it at all!"

What you need
Three play-money dollar bills
Rubber cement

How you fix it
The three bills are cemented together to look like one, forming a flap that is secretly thumbed up or down at the back to make the various changes before turning the bill around.

Put one of the bills on a table, face up, with its long edges top and bottom and with its design right side up. *Carefully* fold it in half from top to bottom, making sure both edges meet exactly, then firmly crease the center fold with your thumbnail and open out the bill again as it was at the start. Liberally coat the top half of it, the entire part above the center fold, with rubber cement.

Take a second face-up bill, turn it so its face design is *upside down,* "standing on its head," and put it squarely on top of the first one. Stick the two together, pressing down so they are tightly cemented, especially around the edges. Wait for the cement to dry. Then carefully fold that second bill from bottom to top, making sure the edges meet, and crease the fold with your thumbnail.

Leave that second one folded in half as it is. Coat the whole surface of both parts with rubber cement, everything that now shows—the folded-up part of the second bill at the top and the unfolded part of the first bill at the bottom. Place the third face-up bill, with its design *right side up,* squarely on top of those and stick them together, again making sure the edges meet exactly and are well cemented. Let the whole thing dry thoroughly before you try using it.

Now hold it up horizontally between your two hands, long edges top and bottom, the face of it toward you, and the back of it toward where the audience would be. Your hands should be at the right and left side edges, fingers in front and thumbs at the back, so the audience will see the whole bill except for the edges you are holding.

Held together that way, it looks like a single bill with front and back designs normally right side up. Still keeping it horizontal, you can turn it around end for end, transferring the right edge to your left hand and left edge to your right hand, or the other way around, to show the back or front of it.

With the face of it toward you, allow the top of it to open slightly, and with your thumbs behind the bill fold the open top part down to the bottom. The face design is now upside down, but the back design is still right side up. If you hold it together at the bottom and turn it around to show the face to the audience, the bill seems to have turned itself upside down. Now hold it with the *back* of the bill toward you and move the flap from bottom to top with your thumbs. A face of the bill shows at both sides.

The folds must be well creased in all directions for this to work easily. Fold the bill in half a dozen or so times each way, top to bottom, back and front, and also in half from left to right and right to left. You should be able to fold it and handle it like an ordinary bill.

When you want to change the face design so it is right side up or upside down, always start with the *face* of the bill toward you; when you want to make the back of it vanish so only faces show, always start with the *back* of the bill toward you.

In this routine, you always turn the bill from right to left to show the face design right side up; left to right to show it upside down. All the moves should be slow and deliberate, so the audience has a chance to take in each change before the next one is made. Doing it slowly also gives you plenty of time to secretly move the flap up or down with your thumbs behind the bill.

To set it up, turn the bill face toward you with the flaps positioned so the back and front designs are both right side up, and fold it in half from left to right. Have it that way in your shirt pocket or the right-hand pocket of your slacks.

What you do

Take the bill from your pocket, unfold it, and hold it horizontally between your hands at the side edges of it, with the face of the bill toward the audience. The first part, folding and then unfolding to turn the design upside down, is a well-known little stunt with a dollar bill. Familiar to many, it is not intended to fool anybody, but merely to build up to what is to come. Here is how it is done:

You are holding the face of the bill toward the audience with the design right side up. Fold the right half of it over to the front, from right to left. Then fold the top half toward you, down to the back. Open out the front half to bring it to the top. Unfold the bill from left to right. The face design, as the audience sees it, is now upside down.

To turn it right side up again, fold the left half of it over to the front, from left to right. Then fold the top half away from you, down to the front. Open out the back half to bring it to the top. Then unfold the bill from right to left. The front design is now right side up, as it was at the start.

"Some of you probably know that little trick," you say. "If you turn it from right to left, it stays head up." Without folding the bill, horizontally turn it around from right to left. Hold it a second and turn it again. Hold it and then turn it once more. That leaves the face of it toward you.

Snap the bill between your hands and remove your right hand for an instant to hold it only with your left hand. Bring your right thumb back to the right top edge, slide your thumb inside the flap, and take the bill again with the right fingers in front as before. Release the top left corner from your left thumb. Behind the bill, slowly turn the flap down to the bottom with your thumbs, and hold it together. The face design is now upside down, but still toward you.

"But if you turn it from left to right," you say, "then it flips itself over—upside down." Turn it horizontally left to right, hold it so the audience can see the change, and then turn it once more. The face is toward you again.

With your thumbs behind the bill, shift the flap from bottom to top, and say, "If you turn it right to left, it's right side up." Turn it and show it. Then turn it again so it faces you. Shift the flap from top to bottom. "But left to right— it's upside down." Turn it left to right and show it upside down.

The back of the bill is now toward you. "Just don't turn it from top to bottom—because that get's very confusing," you say. Behind the bill, bring your thumbs to the bottom, turn the flap to the top, and continue to turn the bill over to the front, from top to bottom, using the fingers of both hands to turn it. Grip it tightly at the bottom, snap it between your hands, and turn it over again from top to bottom, so the audience can see there are only faces on both sides and the back design has disappeared.

Behind the bill, secretly shift the flap from top to bottom. This leaves the front upside down and the back right side up. Turn the bill around horizontally from right to left to show that it has a back design again and it is right side up.

"Turn it from left to right," you say, "and it is upside down." Turn it around from left to right to show the face upside down. Now turn it right to left to show the back still right side up. Secretly shift the flap from bottom to top and say, "But just turn it from right to left and we're back where we started—heads up again." Turn it from right to left and show that the face now also is right side up.

"If that's all clear to you ... I hope somebody will explain it to me." Turn it twice more, right to left, showing that both sides of the bill are normal again, and fold it up and put it away in your pocket as you say, "Because I just don't understand it at all!"

COMEDY CUT BILL

How it looks

You cut a dollar bill in half, hold up the two pieces separately, and then put them together and trim off the cut edges. "Will you just snap your fingers?" you ask someone in the audience. When he does, you shake the bill open to show it is whole once more. "There it is. Just as good as new ..."

But something has gone wrong! The bill is together in one piece, but the two halves are reversed. Half of the back of the bill is joined to half of the face, so the two parts are in opposite directions. "Which hand did you use when you snapped your fingers?" you ask the spectator. When he answers, you say, "No wonder. That was the wrong hand."

COMEDY CUT BILL

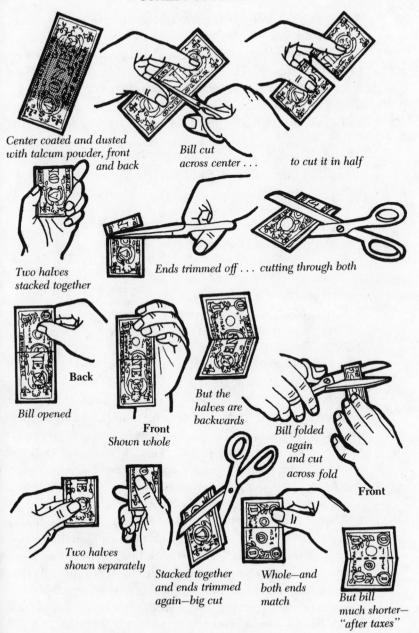

Center coated and dusted with talcum powder, front and back

Bill cut across center . . .

to cut it in half

Two halves stacked together

Ends trimmed off . . . cutting through both

Back

Bill opened

Front
Shown whole

But the halves are backwards

Bill folded again and cut across fold

Front

Two halves shown separately

Stacked together and ends trimmed again—big cut

Whole—and both ends match

But bill much shorter— "after taxes"

You cut the bill apart again, show the two halves, and trim off the cut edges. "Now snap your fingers," you say. "With the other hand." He does and you shake the bill open to show it properly whole again. But it is much smaller than it was at the start because so much has been cut away. "We seem to have lost about forty cents' worth," you say. "But that's how any dollar looks—after taxes."

What you need
A dozen play-money bills
Rubber cement
Talcum powder
An old newspaper
A sharp pair of scissors that will fit into your breast pocket

How you fix it
This is based on an old trick of repeatedly cutting and restoring a strip of paper that has been treated with rubber cement. The pressure of the scissors as they cut through it automatically sticks the cut center edges together so it appears to be whole again.

Since you will cut up one of the bills each time you practice or do the trick, it is easiest to prepare a batch of them all at once. Lay all the bills separately in face-up rows on the opened-out newspaper. Thickly coat the entire center of each bill with rubber cement, right across from side to side, brushing it out to the edges and covering a center area of about 3 inches.

When it is dry, apply a good second coat. Allow the bills to dry again and then spread talcum powder liberally over the coated sections, smoothing it with the tip of your finger. Shake off the excess powder, turn all the bills' backs upward, and repeat the same process, so they are double-coated and powdered at the center on both sides. The supply of bills can be stored in an envelope. Because of the powder, they won't stick together.

Turn one of them with its narrow edges top and bottom, and fold it exactly in half, top to bottom. Have it that way in your breast pocket with the scissors.

What you do
Take out the bill and scissors. Unfold the bill, show it, and hold it with your left hand. With the scissors in your right hand, cut across the center crease to cut the bill in two. Hold one half in each hand, show them, and bring the halves together in your left hand so that the *back* of one half lies squarely against the *face* of the other half, with the cut edges of both at the top.

Trim off the two cut edges together, cutting evenly right across through both, to cut off about ¼ inch. Let the trimmed-off scraps fall to the floor and put the scissors into your breast pocket. Bring your right hand to the bottom edges of the bill and take the outer edge between your right thumb and fingers, still holding the bill with your left hand.

Ask a spectator to snap his fingers. When he does, hold up your right hand so the bill unfolds and hangs open from that hand. Because the rubber cement holds the cut edges, the bill appears to be restored in one piece, but with the two halves reversed, so that one part of it is the face of a bill and the other part the back of a bill.

Stare at the strange-looking bill, then look at the spectator and ask, "Which hand did you use when you snapped your fingers?" Whatever he answers, say, "No wonder. That was the wrong hand."

Bring the palm of your left hand against the bottom part of the bill that is hanging from your right hand and fold the bill shut. Take the scissors from your pocket. Cut right across through both of the two edges together, again trimming away about ¼ inch. Separate the two pieces and show one in each hand.

Now bring them together into your left hand again, one atop the other, but this time so that the two pieces are *face to face* or *back to back*. You can easily arrange that as you show the pieces separately and turn them over. Hold the two together and trim about ½ inch off the already cut edges, cutting evenly through both pieces at once as before. Put the scissors away in your pocket. Holding the bill in your left hand, take the outer bottom edge of it between your right thumb and fingers.

"Now snap your fingers," you tell the spectator. "With the other hand." When he does, hold up the bill with your right hand so it unfolds and hangs open, properly restored but now so much shorter that it looks like a midget-sized bill. Say, "We seem to have lost about forty cents' worth. But that's how any dollar looks—after taxes." Fold the small bill and put it away in your pocket.

IN THE RED

How it looks

"I wonder if money will ever go out of style?" you say, as you take four bills from your pocket and transfer them one at a time from hand to hand, showing both sides of each, their designs the usual black and green. "Some people say that with all the credit cards there are—who needs money?" You hold the packet of bills stacked together. "The trouble is that if you keep buying too many things on credit—sooner or later, you're sure to wind up in the red!"

As you speak, the front bill of the packet suddenly turns red. Then you show that they have all become red, on both sides. "I've heard of dirty money," you say, as you put them back into your pocket, "but did you ever see money *blush* before?"

What you need
Eight play-money bills
A red felt-tip pen
Nonshiny transparent tape

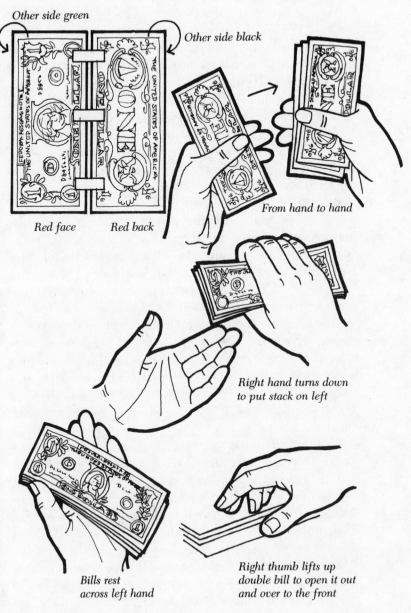

Other side green

Other side black

Red face   Red back

From hand to hand

Right hand turns down
to put stack on left

Bills rest
across left hand

Right thumb lifts up
double bill to open it out
and over to the front

81

How you fix it

With the red pen, color the printed parts of the faces and backs of three of the play-money bills, but leave the borders white. Just run the pen back and forth within the borders, coloring evenly but not too heavily, so the designs still show faintly through the red.

Then color *only the face* of a fourth bill and *only the back* of a fifth bill, leaving the reverse sides of each of those as they are, and again leaving the borders white. Put those two on a table with their red sides up and narrow ends top and bottom. The left one should have its top printed border to the left; the right one its top border to the right.

Bring them vertically together side by side so their long edges almost touch, leaving a space of about 1/16 inch between them. Make sure they are exactly even. Hinge the two together by running three 1½-inch lengths of tape horizontally across from one to the other, one strip near the top, one at the center, one near the bottom. Keep the tiny space between the two bills so the tape hinges won't bind.

Close the left one down upon the right one, as though closing a book, and you should have what looks from both sides like a single ordinary bill. Open them out again and fold the left one the opposite way, around to the back, and you have what looks like a single bill but red on both sides. The folder-like double bill should close easily in either direction.

To set up the trick, open out the double bill so the red parts face you. On the right half of it, place the three bills that are colored red on both sides. Close the double bill from left to right, so the three red ones are inside it, and tap the edges so they are all evenly squared up. Keep the open edges of the double bill toward the right and stack the three ordinary uncolored bills evenly on top of it.

Have them all stacked that way, narrow ends top and bottom, in the inner right-hand pocket of your jacket. (If you wish, you can have them stacked in a secretary-type wallet, the kind that holds bills full-length without folding them.)

What you do

Take the bills from your pocket, keeping them stacked as they are, and tap the edges to even them again, if necessary. Hold them vertically upright in your left hand, narrow ends top and bottom, thumb across the center, and with the back of your hand toward the audience.

Bring your right hand over, its back also to the audience, and thumb the top bill from your left hand into your right, which takes it vertically with its thumb across the center to hold it. Turn your right hand outward to the right to show the other side of the bill to the audience, and then bring it back as it was to take the second one from the left hand.

Thumb the second one off on top of the first one in your right hand, just as though you were dealing cards from the top of a pack, but keep both hands upright. Show both sides of it as before and continue in that way, taking the third on top of the second, and finally taking the double bill as if it were a fourth single one. Transferring them singly from hand to hand has now put the double one on top of the stack, facing you in your right hand.

Hold your left hand palm upward in front of you with the tips of the fingers toward the audience. Turn your right hand over toward you and bring it down to place the stack of bills *horizontally* across your outstretched left hand. The double bill is now at the bottom as they rest upon your left palm, and the open edges of that bill are toward your body. Keep your right hand as it is, with its thumb at the rear and its palm above all the bills.

With your left thumb, bend down the left corner of the bottom bill, which is the lower part of the double bill, to separate it a little from all the others above it. Slide your right thumb into the opening, so it is inside the double bill.

Now lift all the bills above your right thumb straight up

from the rear, then forward together between your thumb and fingers, and over to the front of the whole stack. That brings the stack horizontally upright, with the bottom edge of all the bills touching your left palm, and a red bill has suddenly appeared at the face of the packet.

What it really amounts to is opening up the front half of the double bill and closing it again in the opposite direction. The three all-red bills are now at the front of the stack and the three ordinary uncolored bills are now hidden within the double one, which shows both sides red instead of green and black. That has been done by simply lifting all the bills that were above your thumb and turning them over together from back to front. There is no need to hurry the move; do it openly and casually, as though merely turning over the bills on your left hand.

So far the audience has seen only the one red bill at the face of the packet. Hold them all as they are with your left hand for a moment and remove your right hand to tap the edges and square up the stack. This is important, to make sure the ordinary bills are well concealed within the double red one, so it can be handled again as if it were a single bill.

When they are squared up, hold them with your left hand as you did at the start, vertically upright with their narrow ends top and bottom. Transfer them one at a time from hand to hand as at the beginning, thumbing them off from the left hand into the right. Show the front and back of each bill as you take it, so the audience discovers they have all turned red on both sides, and finally put your "blushing money" back into your pocket.

THE TRAVELING MILLIONAIRE

How it looks

"How would you like to travel all over the country like a millionaire and never have to think about money?" you ask, as you take some strips of newspaper from your pocket, open them out, and count them from hand to hand, showing both sides. "No credit cards. No travelers' checks. Just a few scraps of paper ... and right away, you've got instant money!"

As you speak, you slap the newspaper strips against your other hand and they instantly change to dollar bills, which you show singly, front and back. "Money for plane tickets ... for hotels ... for meals ... for sightseeing ... for souvenirs."

Gathering them together, you say, "I wish I could really do that. But they *are* just scraps of paper." You slap your other hand with them again and the bills suddenly change back into strips of newspaper. Once more, you show them from hand to hand. "I wish somehow, in some way, I could turn them all into money." You shake your head and tuck the paper strips back into your pocket. "But to *really* do that—I'd have to be a magician."

What you need
Six play-money bills
An old newspaper
Liquid adhesive such as white craft glue
A pencil, a ruler, and scissors

How you fix it
You will need six pieces of newspaper, each cut to the *exact* size of one of the bills. Because the dimensions have to be precise, measure one of the bills you have and then use the ruler and pencil to mark out guidelines for cutting the paper strips to that size.

Stack the six newspaper strips evenly together on a table with their narrow ends top and bottom. Measure 1 inch down from the top and at that point draw a very light horizontal pencil line across the first strip of the stack. Fold all six strips together up from the bottom to that line, crease the fold with your thumbnail, and then erase the pencil mark.

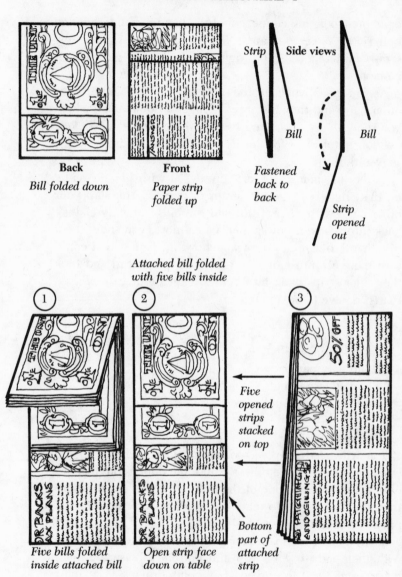

Back

Bill folded down

Front

Paper strip folded up

Strip   **Side views**

Bill

Bill

Fastened back to back

Strip opened out

Attached bill folded with five bills inside

① ② ③

Five opened strips stacked on top

Bottom part of attached strip

Five bills folded inside attached bill

Open strip face down on table

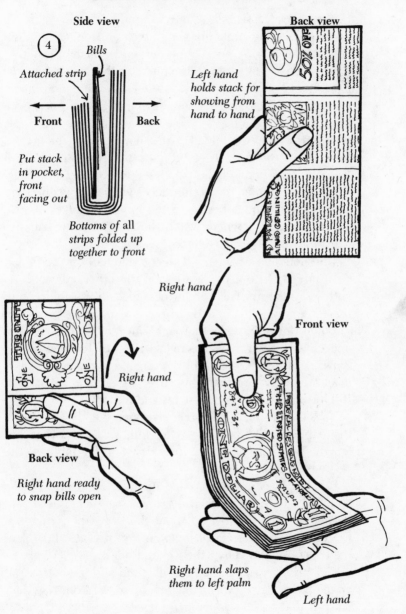

Side view

④

Bills

Attached strip

← **Front**

Back →

Put stack in pocket, front facing out

Bottoms of all strips folded up together to front

Back view

50% OFF

Left hand holds stack for showing from hand to hand

Right hand

Front view

Back view

Right hand ready to snap bills open

Right hand

Right hand slaps them to left palm

Left hand

Now stack the six bills squarely together, narrow ends top and bottom. This time, measure 1 inch up from the bottom edge, draw a faint pencil line across the first bill at that point, and carefully fold all the bills together *down from the top* to that line. Crease the fold and erase the pencil line.

Put five of the bills aside for a moment. Fold the sixth one down from the top on its crease and turn the bill over to its opposite side, so the folded part is underneath, against the table. Coat the surface of the part that now shows with adhesive. Take one of the paper strips, hold it so the part that is folded up at the bottom faces you, and put the strip squarely upon the adhesive-coated bill so all edges exactly match. Press it down to fasten the two together back-to-back, making sure the edges are secure.

You should now have a bill on one side with its top folded down attached to a paper strip on the other side with its bottom folded up. Held one way it looks like a folded bill, the other way like a folded strip of newspaper.

When the adhesive is thoroughly dry, carefully trim any uneven edges with the scissors so none of the newspaper shows at the side with the bill or the other way around. But don't trim off more than tiny slivers because this fake one still has to cover the other strips and bills.

To set it up for the routine, first open out the bottom of the paper strip attached to the bill, so the strip is full length. Turn that open strip face down on the table, so the side with the bill is face up.

Put the five other bills face up inside the fold of the attached one. Fold all the bills down together. Leave that face down as it is. Now open out the five paper strips full length and lay them face down on top of that. Make sure the edges are all even at the top and sides.

Pick up the stack, hold it upright, and fold the bottoms of all the paper strips away from you, up to the front together. Have it that way in your shirt pocket or the breast pocket of your jacket.

What you do

Take it from your pocket with your right hand and hold it vertically in front of you. With your left hand, open out the strips full length. Put your left fingers around the stack at the center and hold it with that hand, with the back of the hand toward the audience and thumb to the rear. Adjust the stack with your right hand to square it up and make sure the bills are covered. Casually turn your left hand out to the left to show the back of the stack and then bring that hand in front of you again.

You now transfer the strips singly from hand to hand to show both sides of them. Bring your right fingers to the top of the stack and separate the first strip at the back, making sure you have only one. Take it with your right hand, show the face of it, turn that hand out to the right to show the back of the strip, and then put it at the *front* of the entire stack and leave it there.

Continue to show each of the others the same way, returning each to the front of the stack your left hand is holding. This moves all the separate strips from the back of the stack to the front of it.

Once or twice, while you are showing a strip with your right hand, let your left hand swing out to the left at the same time, so the audience sees the back of the stack. When you have shown five strips and replaced each at the front, the next one will be the one with the folded bills attached. Leave that on the stack as it is, without removing it. Keep the stack upright and close to you so nobody catches a glimpse of the folded bills at the back.

You are now about to make the bills suddenly appear. Bring your right hand to the stack that your left hand is holding. Fold the bottoms of all the strips up together against the face of the stack. Hold it between your right fingers at the front and thumb at the back, with the thumb just beneath the bottom edge of the folded bills. Bring your left hand in front of your waist, palm up, and swing your right hand over and down to slap the stack against your outstretched left palm. That snaps the bills open so they suddenly unfold full length and come into view.

Immediately take the stack with your left hand, by turning that hand palm downward across the face of the bills, thumb underneath, and lift it to hold the stack vertically upright in front of you. Bring both hands together and spread the bills out in a fan between them, like a fan of playing cards you might be holding in a card game.

With the bills spread out, take the five separate ones with your left hand, put them all *behind* the one remaining in your right hand, and square up the stack. Keep the stack with your left hand, fingers across the front and thumb at the back, and remove your right hand.

You are now set to show the bills one at a time, just as you showed the paper strips at the start. With your right hand, separate one of the bills from the back of the stack, show the bill back and front, and replace it at the *front* of the entire stack. Continue as before until you have shown five of the bills. That leaves the stack ready to change the bills back into paper strips.

You do it exactly the way you first changed the strips into bills. First fold the bottoms of all the bills up together against the face of the stack. Hold the stack with your right-hand fingers at the front and your thumb just beneath the bottom edge of the folded strips at the back. With your right hand, slap the stack down against your outstretched left palm. The strips suddenly snap open full length, so it seems to the audience that the bills visibly change back to strips of paper.

Again take the stack with your left hand down across the face of it, bring it vertically upright in front of you, and spread the strips into a fan between both hands. But this last time keep all the strips as they are at the face of the stack. Square it up, separate one strip from the *front*, show both sides, and put it at the *back* of the stack.

Continue showing the strips singly as you put them from the face to the back, and also occasionally show the back of the stack, until you have shown five of the strips. Then fold the bottoms of all the strips up to the front, put the stack away in your pocket, and say, "But to *really* do that—I'd have to be a magician."

(The routine ends with the stack in its original order, so you won't have to set it all up again for the next time you want to do the trick.)

THE MONEY SPELL

Here is another trick that uses the same basic method as The Traveling Millionaire, but with an entirely different presentation. It is especially effective as a quick opening trick, but is one that can be carried in your pocket, ready to perform at any time.

How it looks

"I'm about to cast a spell," you say as you show some cards with letters of the alphabet on them. Each card has one letter on the front and another on the back, and you spell them aloud as you show the letters, one at a time: "M-A-G-I-C ... M-O-N-E-Y." Holding the cards stacked together in your hand, you say, "That spells 'magic money' ... and here it is!"

You swing the stack of alphabet cards down to tap them against the palm of your other hand and suddenly the cards all change into dollar bills. As you count the bills from hand to hand, showing both sides of them, you say, "M-A-G-I-C ... and that spells 'magic'!"

What you need
Six play-money bills
Two 5 x 8 inch unlined office file cards or other thin cardboard

THE MONEY SPELL

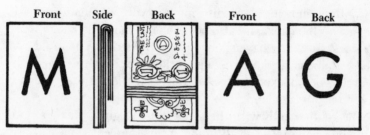

First card, bills folded at back

Five other cards, letters each side: A–G/I–C/M–O/N–E/Y–Blank

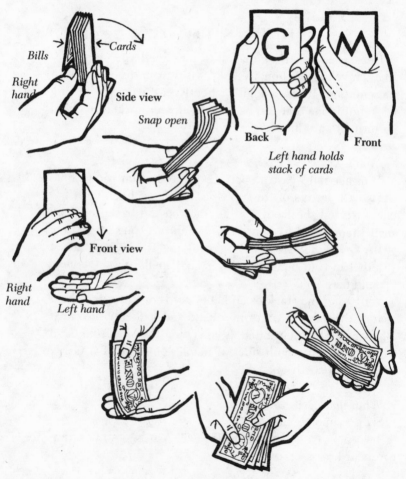

Bills

Cards

Right hand

Side view

Snap open

Left hand holds stack of cards

Back

Front

Front view

Right hand

Left hand

Adhesive such as white craft glue

A rubber band

A black felt-tip pen, a pencil, a ruler, and scissors

How you fix it

The two file cards provide the cardboard for making six small cards, each the *exact* width of the bills and 3¾ inches long. It is easiest to cut one of the small cards first and use that as a pattern for marking out and cutting the others. Since play-money bills vary somewhat in width according to their manufacture, measure the exact width of the bills you are using. Then take one of the file cards and with the pencil and ruler mark off a section exactly that wide and 3¾ inches long. Cut out that small card and use it to mark around so you can cut five more small cards the same size.

Turn one of the bills face down with its narrow edges top and bottom. Coat the face of one of the small cards with white craft glue and fasten that card to the bottom part of the bill so that their edges match squarely at the bottom and both sides.

When the adhesive is dry, turn the bill face up, with the attached card now underneath, against the table. Trim off any tiny edges of the card that may show beyond the edges of the bill. Fold the unfastened top part of the bill down against the face of it, toward the bottom, and crease the fold so the bill is flat.

Now turn the card side of it face up. With the felt-tip pen, print a big block letter "M" on it, filling the face of the card. (You may prefer to use a stencil or stick-on self-adhesive letters.) Take a second card and print a big "A" on its face and a "G" on its back. Print "I" on the face of a third one and "C" on its back. On the opposite sides of a fourth, print "M" and "O," and on a fifth, "N" and "E." Print a "Y" on the face of the last one and leave the back blank.

Turn the card with the attached bill so the bill is facing

you and open out the top fold. Lay the five other bills evenly face up on that one, with all edges matched, and fold them all down from the top together, inside the fold of the attached one. Again crease the fold.

Stack the cards on top in this order, from the bottom up as the letters face you: first the bills, next the blank face, then E, O, C, and G. You may want to pencil small numbers lightly at the upper corners so you will be able to stack them quickly again for later performances.

Square them up, snap the rubber band around them, and have them in the otherwise empty left-hand pocket of your slacks.

What you do

As you say you are about to "cast a spell," take out the cards, remove and discard the rubber band, and hold the stack at its top edge between your right thumb and fingers so the face of the first card can be seen. Show the M at the face of it to the audience, and start spelling aloud, "M . . ."

Leave that card where it is. Bring the palm of your left hand against the face of the stack to hold the cards with that hand, fingers across the front and thumb at the back. With your right hand, take the first card from the *back* of the stack. Hold that one up, long enough for the audience to see the face of it, and spell aloud, "A." Turn that card around to show the back of it and spell, "G."

Now put that card at the *front* of the whole stack in your left hand and leave it there. Take the next one from the back, hold it up and slowly show the letters, first one side and then the other, and spell, "I . . . C." Return that to the front of the others, keeping them all squared up in your left hand as you go along.

Pause a moment and then in the same way—taking each card from the back, holding it up to show one side and then the other, and returning it to the front of the stack—spell out, "M-O-N-E-Y." With the last card, you show the Y at the face of it, turn it around to show that the back of it is blank, and return that to the front of the stack with its blank side still facing the audience.

The folded bills are now at the rear of the stack your left hand is holding. Bring your right hand to the bottom of the stack and take it with that hand, with your four fingers up in front of the bottom edge and thumb at the rear just *below* the edge of the folded-down bills. Hold the stack firmly and keep it upright so nobody glimpses the bills at the back.

Lower your left hand to a level below your waist, turn it palm upward, and hold it outstretched in front of you. Say, "That spells 'magic money' . . . and here it is!" Bring your right hand straight down to the front so the stack lightly slaps against the palm of your left hand and the folded bills snap open. Close your left thumb across the top of the bills and fingers around the side edges to hold the bills and keep them fully opened out. Keep the cards squared in the palm of that hand beneath the bills, which now hide the cards from view, and tilt the hand forward so the front edges of the bills slant slightly toward the floor.

Your left hand is now holding the stack and both hands are still in front of you, down below your waist. With your right hand, separate the first bill from the top of the stack, making sure you have only one. Hold it up, show the audience the front and back of it, and say, "M . . ." Put that back under all the cards and bills in your left hand, sliding it in at the bottom of them, and leave it there. Separate the next bill from the top of the stack, hold it up to show both sides, and say, "A . . ." Return that to the bottom of all the others.

Continue in that way, taking a bill from the top, showing it, saying aloud the next letter, and returning it to the bottom of the stack, just as you naturally would if you were counting a stack of bills. But instead of counting, you spell aloud, "M-A-G-I-C."

(Actually, you count only five bills from hand to hand, leaving the sixth one, which had the card glued to it, on top of the stack at the end. But the spelling aloud of the five-letter word *magic*, while showing a bill for each letter, leads the audience to believe you have shown both sides of all of them. It also leaves the hidden cards sandwiched between the bills, so they are now covered, top and bottom.)

The spelling and counting off of the bills should be done quickly. As you finish the spelling, casually show both sides of the stack of bills in your left hand, and as you fold down the tops of them to put them back into your pocket, say, "And that spells 'magic'!"

HOW TO STRETCH A DOLLAR

How it looks

"I'm going to show you how to double your money," you say as you open out a small piece of cardboard, folded across the center, and show that it is empty. You place a dollar bill against the cardboard, fold the cardboard shut, and then open it to bring out the folded bill, and say, "Already, we've doubled our money."

All you have done is to fold the bill by closing the cardboard with the bill inside it. Continuing to joke about "doubling" the money by folding it, you put the half-folded bill into the cardboard, fold it shut on the bill again, and then take the bill out to show that it has been folded in quarters, and say, "We've doubled it again." You run your fingers along the creased edges of the bill and say, "And if I *crease* it here ... and *crease* it there ... you can see the money *increases*."

The idea has been to lead the audience to think it is just a gag, which makes the magic that is about to happen a more sudden surprise. Twice you have shown the cardboard empty except for the single bill, and your hands also are obviously empty. Closing the cardboard again, you tuck the

HOW TO STRETCH A DOLLAR

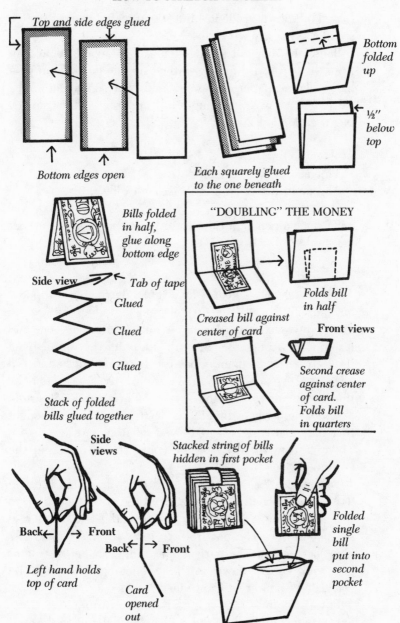

Top and side edges glued

Bottom edges open

Each squarely glued to the one beneath

Bottom folded up

½″ below top

Bills folded in half, glue along bottom edge

Side view

Tab of tape

Glued

Glued

Glued

Stack of folded bills glued together

"DOUBLING" THE MONEY

Creased bill against center of card

Folds bill in half

Front views

Second crease against center of card. Folds bill in quarters

Side views

Back ← → Front

Back ← → Front

Left hand holds top of card

Card opened out

Stacked string of bills hidden in first pocket

Folded single bill put into second pocket

folded bill down inside it. "But if you really want to stretch a dollar," you say, "try this!"

Suddenly you pull a long string of attached dollar bills from the cardboard folder, so they tumble down from your hand like a paper streamer, and you again show the cardboard empty. The single bill apparently has changed into a garland of money.

What you need
Thirteen play-money bills
Three unruled 5 x 8 inch office index file cards
White craft glue
Scissors, a pencil, a ruler, transparent tape, and a rubber band

How you fix it
Put one of the file cards on a table, narrow ends top and bottom, and coat the left, right, and top edges with white glue. Lay a second card squarely on top of the first one and fasten the two together at both sides and the top, leaving the bottom edges open. Coat the two side edges and top edge of the second card in the same way, and fasten the third card on top of the second. Press them all firmly together, and when the glue is dry trim off any tiny edges that may overlap. This gives you what should look like a single card, with two separate compartments open at the bottom edge.

With the ruler, measure ½ inch down from the top and draw a light pencil line across. Fold the bottom edge up to that line, firmly crease the card across the fold, and erase the pencil line. The part folded up at the back is now ½ inch shorter than the part at the front, so when you later put your fingers down into the openings they will be concealed from direct front view.

Put all the bills face up, narrow edges top and bottom. Separately fold each of them in half from top to bottom, horizontally across the center, and crease the folds. Fold *one* of the bills again from top to bottom so it is folded in quarters, crease that fold, and then open out the bill and put it aside. Leave the rest as they are, folded only in half.

Take the first of the remaining twelve folded bills and apply white glue right across its bottom edge, covering an area about ½ inch wide. Put a second folded bill evenly on top of the first one and firmly stick them together, back to back, along the bottom edges. Continue in that way, gluing each folded bill to the one beneath it as you stack them evenly one atop another, until all twelve are attached. As you go along, wipe away any excess glue that may squeeze out from the edges, to keep the free parts of the bills from accidentally sticking together.

Allow the glue to dry thoroughly. Then take a 2-inch length of transparent tape and attach one end of it vertically to the bottom edge of the bill that is at the top of the stack. Fold the tape and attach the other end of it to the underside at that edge, to form a small tab of tape. The tab will help you to find that bill quickly, without fumbling, when you later produce the bills.

The result should be an accordion-like string of bills. If you take the tab of the top one with your right hand and lift your arm as high as you can, the rest will unfold to hang down in a string. Put the palm of your left hand beneath the bottom bill of the string and slowly bring your hands together, and they will all fold together again into a stack.

To set things up for the trick, first turn the stack of bills so that all the folds are at the bottom and the bill with the tab is facing you, tab at the top. Hold the folded card upright, with the shorter part to the rear and open edges at the top. Open out the *front* compartment and slide the stack of bills all the way down into it so they are hidden inside, tab still at the top and toward the back.

Open out the card and put the separate unfolded bill in it, so it lies horizontally across the inside center of the card,

with the two ends of the bill sticking out from the sides. Close the card, snap the rubber band vertically around it, and have it on your table with the open edges toward the back and the shorter part at the bottom.

What you do

Hold the card upright with your right hand and bring your left hand over to take it at the top. Put your left thumb at the back, first finger down inside the center and other fingers at the front. Press your thumb and first finger together to keep the top opening of the shorter part shut. Your left hand will hold the card at the top that way until the end of the trick.

With your right hand, remove the rubber band and put it on the table. Then take the edge of the bill with that hand, draw it out, and open the card as your left fingers release the front part so it can be opened. With your left hand, casually turn the card to show the front and back of it. Tell the audience, "I'm going to show you how to double your money."

Hold the bill vertically against the face of the card, so the bill's center crease is at the card's center fold. Close up the front of the card, which folds the bill in half; then open the card again and take out the folded bill to show it as you joke, "Already, we've doubled our money." Put the second crease of the bill against the card's center, close the card and open it, and show the now doubly folded bill. "We've doubled it again."

Close up the front of the card and keep it closed with your left hand. Holding the twice-folded bill with your right hand, touch your finger to its edges as you joke, "And if I *crease* it here and *crease* it there . . . you can see the money *increases*."

Bring the folded bill to the top of the card. With your right fingers, pull open the *back* compartment of the card. Slide the folded bill into it and push it down until it is hidden inside. You can do this quite deliberately, with no need to hurry, since the top openings are hidden from front view by the longer part of the card that is folded up at the front. It looks as if you are merely pulling open the folded card at the top so as to slide the bill down into the center of it.

"But if you really want to stretch a dollar," you say, "try this!" Reach down into the *front* compartment, grip the tape tab firmly between your right thumb and first finger, and lift your arm straight up into the air, pulling the whole stack of bills out of the card so they fall open and hang down from your right hand.

Display the string of bills for a moment. Then open out the card with your left hand to show that it is empty and bring it beneath the bottom bill of the string, so that bill rests upon the card. Slowly lower your right hand to let the bills fold again into a stack as your hands come together. Close the card with the stack of bills inside it, pick up the rubber band from the table, snap it around the card, and put it away in the inside pocket of your jacket.

4

SHOWTIME TRICKS
WITH MONEY

PENETRATING COINS AND PURSE

How it looks

You take a small change purse from your pocket, casually show both sides of it, open the purse, and tip four half-dollars out into your hand. One at a time, you put the coins back into the purse and show that both hands are otherwise empty.

Taking the purse in one hand, you pick up a glass from the table with your other hand. You strike the top of the glass sharply with the purse, and one of the coins seems to pass right through the closed purse to fall with a clink into the glass. When you open the purse and pour the coins from it, there are only three. One by one, you pass the remaining coins from the purse into the glass in the same way.

What you need

A small imitation leather change purse, about 2½ inches

PENETRATING COINS AND PURSE

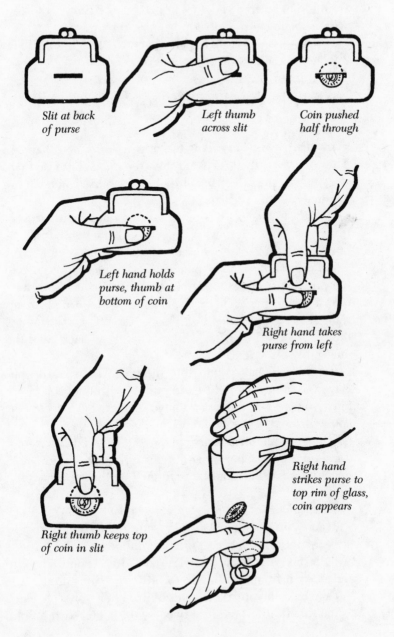

Slit at back
of purse

Left thumb
across slit

Coin pushed
half through

Left hand holds
purse, thumb at
bottom of coin

Right hand takes
purse from left

Right thumb keeps top
of coin in slit

Right hand
strikes purse to
top rim of glass,
coin appears

103

from top to bottom and 4 inches across the center, the kind with a single clasp that snaps shut at the top

A straight-sided drinking glass, about 4½ inches high and 3 inches in diameter across the top

Four half-dollars

A sharp-pointed pair of scissors, a pencil, and a ruler

How you fix it

In this trick, what seems to happen really does happen. The coins actually do pass through the purse, because there is a slit cut across the back of it—but the purse and coins are handled so as to hide that.

Lay the purse on the table with its top pointed away from you. With the ruler, measure 1 inch up from its bottom edge, and at a point centered from the left and right edges draw a horizontal pencil line 1½ inches long. Hold the purse open so as not to cut the opposite side, carefully push through the point of the scissors, and cut a clean slit right along the penciled line. (In the directions that follow, the slit side of the purse will be called the "back" and the uncut side the "front.")

Put the four half-dollars into the purse and snap it shut. Have the purse in a right-hand pocket with the back of the purse toward your body, and have the glass on a table that you will stand beside while performing.

(This is a "platform" trick, planned to be used as part of a stand-up magic show; it is not for close-up performance, since the purse must not be examined by the spectators.)

What you do

Reach into your pocket with your right hand, grip the purse at its top between your thumb and first finger, and bring it out with its back toward you. Hold it up to show it and shake it from side to side to rattle the coins inside it.

Take it from your right hand by bringing your left hand to the side of it to hold it between your fingers at the front and your thumb just beneath the slit at the back. With your right hand, unsnap the purse and open it wide, then bring that hand down cupped beneath it.

Tip the purse over from left to right with your left hand, still keeping the slit side toward you, and shake the coins out into your cupped right hand. Turn your left hand over from right to left to bring the purse upright again and hold it that way.

Count out the coins from your right hand by dropping them, one at a time, flat onto the table. Then pick one up, hold it between your thumb and first finger, and put it into the purse in your left hand. As you put the coin down inside, push the bottom edge of it through the slit so that part of the coin comes out at the back under your left thumb, which holds it there against the back of the purse.

With your right hand, pick up another coin from the table, show it, and put that into the bottom of the purse. Continue until all four are in the purse and then snap it shut.

Show your right hand empty and bring it down over the top of the purse that is still in your left hand. With your right thumb and fingertips pointed downward, take hold of the top of the purse between them, fingers at the front and thumb at the back. The tip of your right thumb should be just *above* the slit. Press your thumb against the purse there to keep the coin in the slit from falling all the way out, and take your left hand away from the purse.

You are now holding the purse with your right hand at the top. At the back of the purse there is a coin halfway through the·slit, with the top half of that coin still inside the purse, kept there by the pressure of your thumb.

Take the glass from the table with your left hand around the back of it near the bottom and hold it firmly out in front of you at waist level.

With your right hand, bring the purse down quickly against the top rim of the glass, rather flat and with the back of the purse at a downward angle. Release the pressure of your right thumb on the coin and it will fly from the slit to strike the inside of the glass and clink down into it.

Hold up the glass, rattle the coin inside it, and put the glass on the table. Transfer the purse to your left hand, which takes it by the side, fingers in front and thumb against the slit at the back. Open the top clasp with your right hand and then hold that hand cupped beneath.

With your left hand, tip the purse from left to right, still keeping the back of it toward you, and pour the coins from it into your cupped right hand. Drop them one at a time onto the table to show there were only three left in the purse.

All of this takes only a few moments, and with the purse in your left hand and three coins on the table you are now ready to repeat it again, by singly putting the three coins into the purse, striking the glass, and passing another one through. Then you put two coins into the purse and pass one of them into the glass. Each time you do it, the coin that falls into the glass is left there.

Finally, you put the fourth coin into the purse and pass that into the glass. When you reach that point, transfer the purse from your right hand to your left, taking it with your left hand at the side of it, fingers in front and thumb against the slit at the back. With your right hand, unsnap it and open the top wide. Turn your left hand over from left to right to tip the purse upside down, shake it to show it is empty, and turn your hand right to left to bring the purse upright again.

Take the glass with your right hand and spill the four coins out flat onto the table. Gather them up, bring that hand above the mouth of the purse, and drop them down into it one at a time. Snap it shut, rattle the coins in it with your left hand, and put the purse away in your left-hand pocket.

THE CONTRARY COINS

How it looks

"Four silver coins," you say as you point to a row of coins displayed on a small cardboard stand. You show your hands empty and gather up the coins. "For this trick, it is very important to have exactly four." You start counting them aloud, from hand to hand: "One, two, three, four . . . *five?*"

You pretend to be surprised to discover that you suddenly have a fifth coin. "That's funny—where did that come from?" You toss the extra coin aside on the table and put the other four back in a row on the stand. "I'm sorry. I'll try that again. . . . Exactly four silver coins." Gathering them up, you count them from hand to hand, and discover that this time you have two extra coins: "One, two, three, four . . . *five, six?*"

You throw the extra two on the table, put four back on the stand, gather them up, count them from hand to hand, and discover that you have seven: "One, two, three, four . . . *five, six . . . seven?*"

With mock annoyance, you toss all the coins onto the table, brush your hands together, and say, "Forget it! The more money I throw away, the more I've got. . . . If I keep this up, I'll turn into a millionaire!"

What you need

Ten half-dollars

A piece of white poster board, cut to a size of 5½ × 10 inches

White plastic adhesive tape, ¾ inch wide

Two white envelopes, each 4⅛ × 9½ inches (standard business-letter size)

A ruler, a pencil, and scissors

THE CONTRARY COINS

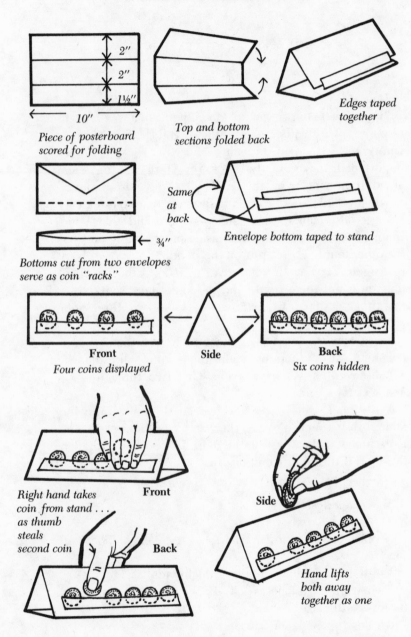

2"
2"
1½"

10"

Piece of posterboard
scored for folding

Top and bottom
sections folded back

Edges taped
together

Same
at
back

Envelope bottom taped to stand

¾"

Bottoms cut from two envelopes
serve as coin "racks"

Front
Four coins displayed

Side

Back
Six coins hidden

Right hand takes
coin from stand . . .
as thumb
steals
second coin

Front

Back

Side

Hand lifts
both away
together as one

108

How you fix it

The secret is in the coin stand, which is easily made by forming the poster board into a long triangle. Simple in appearance, it has the advantage of not looking like a "tricky" prop, but extra coins can be hidden along the back of it so you can secretly add them to those that your hand openly takes from the front.

To make the stand, first turn the piece of poster board lengthwise, long edges top and bottom. Measure 1½ inches up from the bottom edge and draw a pencil line across from one side to the other. Now measure 2 inches up from the line you have just drawn and pencil another line straight across. Hold the ruler in place and run the point of the scissors along each line to score them for easy folding.

Fold the top and bottom sections back away from you along the scored lines, crease the folds with your thumb and fingers, and form the board into a long upright triangle. Cut a 10-inch length of white plastic adhesive tape and fasten the two open edges of the triangle together where they meet, running the tape along so its width overlaps to bind them securely. The result should be a triangular stand 10 inches long that will rest by itself on its 1½-inch base, with slanted 2-inch panels at the front and back.

Two long and narrow envelope-like pockets serve as "racks" to hold the coins on the stand. They are made from the bottoms of the two envelopes. Turn both envelopes lengthwise and measure ¾ inch up from the bottom of each and draw a line across. Cut off those bottom sections and discard the remainder of the envelopes.

Very lightly pencil a guideline across the front panel of the stand, ½ inch up from its bottom edge. Take one of the cut-off envelope bottoms, open it out a little, and fasten a 9-inch length of white plastic tape along its entire top *inside* edge so that half the width of the tape sticks to the inside. Position the envelope piece with its bottom edge along the penciled guideline, center it from the sides, and fasten it to the front of the stand by pressing the tape firmly into place. Attach the second envelope piece to the back panel of the stand in a similar way, again with its bottom edge ½ inch up from the bottom of the stand.

Put four coins along the front of the stand, spaced out in a row to display them. The bottom edges of the coins rest in the envelope "rack" so that the coins lean back flat against the stand, with most of each coin in full view. Space out the six other coins in a row at the back of the stand where they will be hidden from front view. Have the stand that way on your table.

What you do

Position yourself at the back and slightly to the right of the table. Point to the coins displayed on the stand, and say, "Four silver coins."

Show both hands empty and then bring your right hand down over the top of the stand to start gathering up the coins. With the back of that hand toward the audience, fingertips pointing downward and thumb to the rear, place your fingers over the first coin in the row at the front, and draw it up and away from the stand between your fingers and thumb. Keeping that coin, move your hand along to the next coin in the front row, bringing your hand down over the stand with your fingers in front and thumb at the rear as before.

You will find that as your fingers come over the coin at the front, your thumb comes against a coin at the back of the stand. This is almost automatic because of the way the front and back of the triangular stand slant toward each other. If you pinch your thumb and fingers together as you draw your hand upward, the coin from the front of the stand and the coin at the back will slide up together so you can take them both as one.

It looks as if you are just taking the coin from the front, but you secretly steal the extra coin from the back at the same time. You now really have three coins in your hand instead of the two the audience has seen you take from the front of the stand. Without pausing, move your hand along to take the third visible coin from the row at the front, and then along again to take the fourth one.

"For this trick, it is very important to have exactly four," you now say, and you start counting them aloud as you drop them one at a time from your right hand into your unturned left hand. "One, two, three, four . . ." Pretending surprise, you discover you have a fifth coin and raise your voice questioningly as you say, "*Five?*" Hold that one up between your right first finger and thumb, stare at it, and say, "That's funny. Where did that come from?"

With a shrug, toss it aside flatly onto the table, and then dump the others from your left hand into your right. Put the four out along the front of the stand again, spaced so they are opposite coins hidden at the back. "I'm sorry. I'll try that again," you say, pointing to the coins on the stand. "Exactly four silver coins."

Show your hands empty and bring your right hand down over the stand as before and take the first one from the front. Move your hand along to take the second, but as you take it, steal a coin from the back with your thumb. Take a third coin from the front and steal another along with it from the back. Without hesitating, gather up the fourth from the front. Apparently you have just gathered up the four from the front, but you actually have six.

Again count them aloud as you drop them singly from your right hand into your left: "One, two, three, four . . ." Discover that you have another. "*Five?*" Hold it up as you stare at it. Drop it flat onto the table. Then discover that you have still another. "*Six?*" Shake your head and drop that one flat onto the table.

Now quicken the pace. Drop the remaining four coins from your left hand into your right. With your right hand, put them in a row on the stand so that three of them are opposite the three coins still hidden at the back. One coin at the front will have no coin directly behind it. This is the one you take first as you gather them up again. Then move your right hand to the right side of the stand to take the second coin and also steal the one behind it, lifting both together. Move your hand along to take the third and fourth ones from the front, each time also taking one from behind.

Count them from hand to hand: "One, two, three, four . . ." Raise your voice as you discover you have more, and throw those forcefully one at a time into your other hand. "*Five . . . six . . . seven?*" Spill them all out flat across the table from your left hand and brush your hands together. "Forget it! The more money I throw away, the more I've got. . . . If I keep this up, I'll turn into a millionaire!"

THE UNBORROWED COIN IN THE BALL OF WOOL

A popular trick with old-time magicians was the finding of a vanished coin securely wrapped in a box inside a ball of wool. Included in beginners' sets of magic tricks and often explained in print, this classic of coin magic has been somewhat neglected in recent years because the secret use of a small metal slide to get the coin into the ball of wool became too well known. Here is a version that may fool those who know the old secret and that should amuse modern audiences, many of whom have never seen the ancient trick.

How it looks

"Have you ever learned to knit?" you ask a male spectator invited to help you. "So many men as well as women have taken up knitting as a hobby that I just wondered if you were an expert. . . . What I want to show you is a little trick my grandmother taught me to do with a ball of wool. She was not only a knitter. . . . She was also a magician."

THE UNBORROWED COIN IN THE BALL OF WOOL

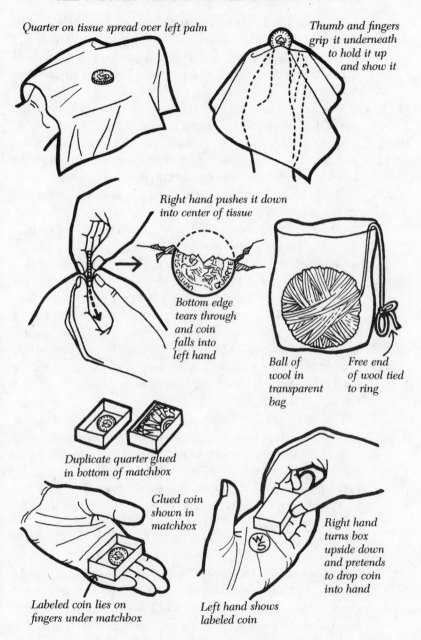

Quarter on tissue spread over left palm

Thumb and fingers grip it underneath to hold it up and show it

Right hand pushes it down into center of tissue

Bottom edge tears through and coin falls into left hand

Ball of wool in transparent bag

Free end of wool tied to ring

Duplicate quarter glued in bottom of matchbox

Glued coin shown in matchbox

Right hand turns box upside down and pretends to drop coin into hand

Labeled coin lies on fingers under matchbox

Left hand shows labeled coin

You show a small transparent bag with a little bright-colored ball of wool inside it. "Don't worry.... You won't have to knit anything. But will you please take charge of this ball of wool and put it away in one of your pockets for now?"

You fold up the bag with the wool in it and give it to him to put into his pocket. "Here's a quarter with a paper label stuck to the back of it so you can write your initials on it," you say, as you show the coin and hand it to him, along with a pen, and ask him to write his initials on the label.

While he is doing that, you open out a facial tissue and spread it over the palm of your hand, then ask him to place the initialed quarter on the tissue. You carefully wrap it in the tissue and give him the small bundle to hold.

"Granny always used to warn me to keep my money in a safe place.... She kept hers under the mattress. But for added security, we'll just use a rubber band." You give him a rubber band and ask him to snap it around the bundle of tissue. "Now you have my money, with your initials on it—and you also have my bag of wool. If you were my grandmother, I'd suspect you were about to knit a magic spell.... Do you mind if I have one last look at my money?"

You take back the tissue and tear it to shreds, which you toss aside. "The quarter's gone—just as I suspected," you say. "Are you sure you never met my grandmother? Do you still have the wool? ... Will you take it from your pocket, please? Just hold the plastic bag at the top—and give me that little ring that has the end of the wool tied to it. Hold the bag tight."

Pulling out the end of the yarn, you quickly draw it from the transparent bag, gathering it up in strands, so the audience can see the ball of wool bouncing around inside the bag as it unravels. A folded envelope comes into view, wrapped at the center of the wool. When you have drawn out the last of the wool, you ask the spectator to remove the envelope from the bag and unfold it. "Is the envelope sealed?" you ask. "Here's a pair of scissors. Will you please cut open the envelope and take out whatever you find inside it?"

He finds a matchbox in the envelope. You take the matchbox, place it on the palm of your hand, and carefully remove the cover. "What do you see inside the box?" He sees a quarter. You dump it out on your hand. "And on the back of the quarter, there's a label with initials on it," you say, as you hold out the quarter to him. "Will you please say whether those initials are yours?"

The spectator confirms that the initials are his, and as you thank him, you say, "I don't know how good you are at knitting . . . but as a magician, Granny would have been proud of you."

What you need
Two quarters that look somewhat alike

A pocket-sized wooden matchbox, the kind with a drawer and sliding cover

A skein of rug yarn, red, blue, green, or some other bright color

A transparent plastic sandwich bag

An envelope

A small plastic ring, such as a curtain ring

A standard-size facial tissue

A self-adhesive paper label, cut to a size slightly smaller than a quarter

A pair of scissors small enough to fit inside your jacket pocket

Several rubber bands

A felt-tip pen

White craft glue or other strong adhesive

How you fix it
Remove the drawer from the matchbox and glue one of the quarters, *face up*, inside the bottom of the drawer, at one end of it. When the glue is thoroughly dry, slide the

drawer back into its cover. Attach the self-adhesive paper label to the *back* of the other quarter and put that aside for a moment.

Put the matchbox into the envelope, seal the envelope, and fold it compactly around the matchbox. Fold it as small as you can.

Cut off a string of yarn about 7 yards long. The length doesn't have to be exact, but if you use a longer piece the later unwinding of it slows the pace of the trick and delays the climax.

Take one end of the yarn, wrap it around the folded envelope, and continue winding it, first in one direction and then another, until you form a tight ball of wool entirely covering the enveloped matchbox at its center. When you come to the end of the yarn, tie that end tightly to the plastic ring. Drop the little ball of wool into the transparent sandwich bag and pull out the free end with the ring attached so that it hangs down at the front of the bag.

Fold the tissue and put that into the right-hand pocket of your jacket. Put the pen and the quarter with the label attached into the same pocket. Have the scissors and rubber bands in the left-hand pocket. Put the bag with the ball of wool in it on the table you will use when performing.

What you do

Pick up the bag and explain that it has a ball of wool in it as you show it to the audience and to the spectator. Fold the bag around the wool and ask the spectator to put it into one of his pockets.

Take the quarter from your right-hand pocket. Hold up the coin to show it, turn it to show the paper label attached to the back of it, and hand it to the spectator. Ask him to write his initials on the label, and reach into your right-hand pocket again and take out the pen and facial tissue. Give him the pen and shake open the tissue. Bring your left palm upward in front of you and spread the opened tissue over the palm of that hand.

When he has written his initials, take back the pen with your right hand and put it away in your pocket. Ask him to place the quarter on the tissue. Grip it through the tissue from underneath, between the tip of your left thumb at the back and tips of your fingers in front, and hold the coin upright by its bottom edge. Display it that way so everybody can see it at the center of the tissue.

The bottom edge of the coin now rests in a little fold of tissue between your thumb and fingertips. Bring your right hand to the top edge of the upright coin and push it down as though pushing it into that fold. But really push it right down *through* the tissue so that the coin falls into your left hand, which is still covered by the tissue. This takes hardly any pressure, since the bottom edge of the pushed-down coin easily tears through the bottom of the tissue fold that is gripped between your thumb and fingers.

With both hands still together, fold up the tissue with your right hand as though the coin were inside it, bunching it into a wad with the torn part in the center. Close your left fingers around the coin to hide it, and take the wadded tissue with your right hand to hold it up and show it as you let your left hand fall to your side with the concealed coin.

Give the wadded tissue to the spectator. Then say that "for added security, we'll use a rubber band." Put your left hand into your left pocket. Leave the coin in the bottom of the pocket, bring out a rubber band, and give it to the spectator as you ask him to snap it around the bundled tissue.

"Now you have my money, with your initials on it—and you also have my bag of wool," you say. "If you were my grandmother, I'd suspect you were about to knit a magic spell. . . . Do you mind if I have one last look at my money?"

Take the tissue from him, remove the rubber band, and toss it aside. Hold the wadded tissue in full view, gripped between the thumbs and fingers of both hands, and suddenly pull your hands apart, tearing the tissue in two.

With repeated pulls, quickly tear it into shreds, then throw them all into the air and let them flutter down to the floor as you show both hands empty, and say, "The quarter's gone—just as I suspected."

(This convincing vanish of a coin can be used in other tricks. It provides more dramatic action, something more for the audience to see, than if you merely vanished a coin from a handkerchief or in some other standard way. Ripping the tissue to shreds also destroys the evidence that it was already torn.)

Ask the spectator to take out the bag with the little ball of wool in it, which he has had in his pocket since the start of the trick. Have him unfold the bag and hold it open by its top edge so the bag hangs down from his hand. Make sure he holds it tight. Take the plastic ring that is tied to the end of the yarn, draw it *up* and step back a few feet, so the audience has a clear view of the bag.

Hold your right hand high and pull the wool *up* out of the bag, using your other hand to quickly gather it as the ball unravels and the envelope at its center comes into view inside the bag. Put the gathered wool aside on the table, have him remove the envelope, and take the empty bag from him and put that aside.

Ask him if the envelope is sealed and say you will give him a pair of scissors to cut it open. Reach into your pocket with your left hand. Get the coin into your fingers and feel it to make sure the side with the paper label faces *upward*. Finger-palm it that way, or simply close your lower three fingers loosely around it to hide the coin. Take the scissors between your thumb and first finger and bring them out of your pocket. Transfer the scissors to your right hand and let your left hand, with the coin hidden in it, fall to your side.

Hand him the scissors and ask him to cut open the envelope. Take back the scissors with your right hand and put them on the table. After he has removed the matchbox from the envelope, take it from him with your right hand

and hold it up to show it, fingers wide apart so it can be seen that there is nothing else in your hand.

Bring your left hand up in front of you, slightly cupped toward you and with the back of it to the audience. Put the matchbox into your left hand, right on top of the hidden coin so it covers it, and hold your left hand out flat to show the matchbox resting on it. With your right first finger, push the drawer of the matchbox open a little. Slide back the cover, remove it, and keep it in your right hand. This leaves the drawer of the matchbox lying on your left fingers, hiding the coin beneath it. Inside the drawer is the face-up duplicate coin that was glued there.

Hold out your left hand and ask the spectator what he sees in the box. When he answers that there is a quarter in it, say, "And on the back of it there's a label, with initials on it." With your right hand, turn the drawer over upside down, as if dumping the glued coin out of it into your left hand. Immediately lift the drawer away, still upside down, and show him the labeled coin on your left hand. Hold it out so he can take the coin and ask him to say whether the initials are his.

While he is doing that, casually put the matchbox and cover away in your right-hand pocket. When he has confirmed the initials, thank him and say, "I don't know how good you are at knitting . . . but as a magician, Granny would have been proud of you."

CATCHING COINS FROM THE AIR

Few classics of coin magic have more audience appeal than the catching of coins from the air, which combines sight, sound, and action with the magical wish fulfillment of seeming to produce money from nowhere. Here is a short, direct version with an updated plot, and a simple device that converts an ordinary metal can into a self-contained prop for delivering coins as you need them.

CATCHING COINS FROM THE AIR

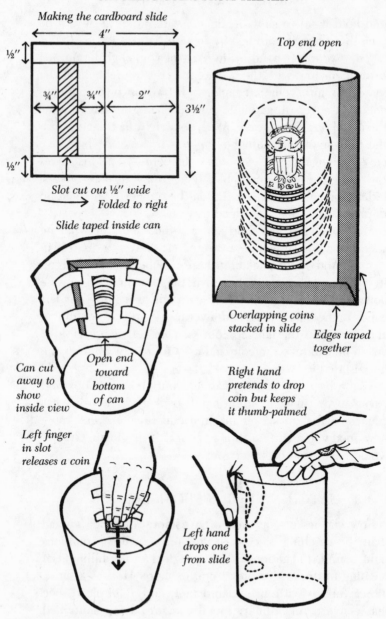

Making the cardboard slide

4"

½"

¾" ¾" 2"

3½"

Slot cut out ½" wide
Folded to right

Slide taped inside can

Top end open

Overlapping coins
stacked in slide

Edges taped
together

Can cut
away to
show
inside view

Open end
toward
bottom
of can

Left finger
in slot
releases a coin

Right hand
pretends to drop
coin but keeps
it thumb-palmed

Left hand
drops one
from slide

120

How it looks

"Everybody these days seems to be worrying about taxes—and with good reason," you say, as you show both hands empty and pick up a large metal can. "But I think I have a way to solve the whole problem."

You hold the can upside down to convince the audience there is nothing in it and then take it with your left hand. "All the government has to do is hire a bunch of magicians as tax collectors and put them to work in Washington, collecting the taxes by plucking the money right out of the air—in the form of cold, hard cash."

Reaching out with your right hand, you seem to catch a coin from the air, then you drop it into the can where it lands with a loud clink. You tip it out of the can into your right hand to display it and then drop it back into the can. "There's the sales tax." Another coin appears at your fingertips and you drop that into the can. "Property tax . . ."

One at a time, you produce coins from behind your knee, your ear, beneath your elbow, the heel of your shoe, dropping each into the can. "Excise tax . . . luxury tax . . . income tax . . . *thumb tacks?*"

You catch another at your fingertips as you say, "Wouldn't that be a lot easier than all the red tape we go through filling out tax forms and everything? Just reach out . . . and you've got it."

Holding that coin well above the can, you let it drop down into it, and show your hand empty. Then you sweep your hand through the air, close your fingers and catch still another, which you drop into the can. "Almost any tax collector could be taught to do it. It wouldn't take any long government training program. Anybody could learn—with the help of a little magic."

You look out toward some person in the audience. "There's one floating past you, sir. As it comes past, will you just reach out and close your hand around it? . . . Now throw it back, please." You hold up the can to "catch" the invisible coin as the person pretends to throw it, and it is heard to land inside the can. "Thank you. There's no use trying to hold out on the tax collector, you know."

Tipping the can over, you spill all the coins out into your hand, then dump them back into the can with a clatter. "As every taxpayer knows," you say, "this is called paying through the nose. . . ." You bring your hand up to your nose and a sudden shower of coins seems to pour down from your nose into the can.

You rattle the coins, put the can back on the table, and say, "Thank you all for paying your taxes so promptly. . . . I'll take this over to the tax office right after the show."

What you need

Ten half-dollars

A large fruit-juice or tomato-juice can, about 7 inches high and 4¼ inches in diameter, washed and dried, with the top cleanly removed so there are no rough edges and the label peeled off

A small piece of poster board, cut to a size of 3½ × 4 inches

Cloth or plastic adhesive tape, ¾ inch wide

A pencil, scissors, and a ruler

How you fix it

As in most versions of the coin-catching trick, this one depends upon repeatedly producing the same coin with the right hand, which only pretends to drop it into the can but really keeps it thumb-palmed so that the same coin can be made to appear at the fingertips again. Each time the right hand pretends to drop a coin, the left hand releases a coin so it clinks into the bottom of the can that hand is holding. The sound convinces the audience that the right hand has dropped its coin into the can.

When this is done entirely by sleight of hand, it requires

secretly "stealing" a stack of coins from some hiding place with the left hand and then quietly getting them into the can in position for releasing them one at a time. To eliminate the need for that, this routine uses a slotted tube-like slide, formed of the small piece of poster board, which is fastened inside the top of the can to hold ten overlapping coins.

At the start, the coin-loaded can is upside down on the table, so the interior is hidden from view even if the audience is fairly close. Both hands start completely free of any hidden coins and the inverted can may be handled casually without any worry that the coins may rattle or spill out as long as it is kept bottom up. As soon as the left hand takes the can and turns it upright, the coins are set to be released one at a time.

To make the slide, start by placing the piece of poster board lengthwise on a table. At its center, 2 inches in from each side, draw a vertical pencil line, from top to bottom. Run the point of the scissors down that line to scribe it for later folding.

On the part that is to the left of that center line, draw two horizontal lines, the first ½ inch down from the top and the second ½ inch up from the bottom. Now draw two vertical lines, one ¾ inch in from the left and the other ¾ inch in from the right. Cut out and remove the section between the two vertical lines so that you have an open slot ½ inch wide, starting ½ inch down from the top and ending ½ inch up from the bottom.

Fold the left half of the whole piece squarely down upon the right half, along the scribed center line, as if closing a book. Bind the right edges together by attaching half the width of a strip of cloth tape to the front and folding it around to the back. With another strip of tape, bind the bottom edges together, but leave the top end open.

That completes the making of the slide, but it has to be

opened out a little so the coins will slide freely. Hold its side edges between your thumb and fingers and squeeze inward so as to billow out the front and rear, flexing it until the top end remains open. It is now ready to fix into place inside the can.

Rest the can on its side on the table, mouth toward you. Lay the poster-board slide vertically inside the can, with the open end of it toward the can's bottom and the closed end about an inch down from the top rim. Fasten it securely in that position with four 2-inch lengths of tape, two at the top and two near the bottom, by sticking one end of each piece of tape to the outer edge of the slide and pressing the rest of it onto the inside of the can.

The coins now have to be loaded into the slide. With your left hand, hold the can up by its side so the mouth of it is tilted slightly toward you. Take one of the coins with your right hand and insert a side edge of it into the center slot, then slide it forward a little until you can get its opposite edge into the slot. When both edges of the coin are inside the slot, draw it back toward you to the top of the slide.

Insert the edge of a second coin into the slot, push it forward until both edges are inside, and again draw it toward you until it partly overlaps the face of the first coin. Continue to insert the rest of the coins the same way, each partly overlapping the one beneath. Adjust them with your fingertip in the slot so they overlap evenly.

This is explained in detail because the coins cannot be properly positioned by putting them in through the open end of the slide; they must be inserted singly through the center slot. After you use it a few times, the poster board will become quite flexible and you will find you can load all ten coins quickly and easily.

When the can is loaded with all ten, turn the mouth of it toward the floor. Hold it so the part with the slide is to the rear and rest it that way, bottom up, on the table you will use when performing.

What you do

Let it be seen that both hands are empty and bring your right hand over the inverted can to pick it up by the bottom rim between your fingers at the front and thumb at the back. Take it from the table, still bottom up, and let your hand fall to your side with it, which is silent "proof" to the audience that the upside down can must be empty. Step away from the table as you talk about taxes and say that you have a way to solve the problem. At this point, both hands are at your sides.

Bring the can in front of your legs to take it from your right hand with your left, by turning your left hand palm upward so its four fingers go up inside the can and cover the slide, with the rim of the can at the crotch of your thumb and the thumb at the outside. Press the tip of your left second finger through the slot to hold the coins in the slide, and as you take the can, let your left hand fall naturally to your side again. That automatically turns the can upright, mouth to the top.

Say that if the government hired magicians as tax collectors, they could pluck the taxes "right out of the air—in the form of cold, hard cash." Then reach out with your right hand as if to catch a coin from the air. Close your fingers around the imaginary coin, hold the can up with your left hand, and pretend to drop the coin into it from your right hand by bringing that hand into the top of the can. With your left hand, release the first coin from the slide so it falls clinking into the bottom of the can as though it were the coin your right hand dropped.

Rattle the can and then tip it over toward the right to slide that coin out into your right hand. Say, "There's the sales tax." As you hold the coin up to show it with your right hand, bring it into position for thumb-palming, clipped at your fingertips between the sides of your first and second fingers. (For a detailed explanation, see the section called "The Thumb-Palm: Fingertip Vanish" in chapter 1.)

Pretend to drop the coin back into the can, but thumb-palm it as your hand goes down inside, and with your left hand release another coin from the slide so it falls to the bottom of the can. Immediately lift your apparently empty right hand away, with its coin thumb-palmed, and let it fall to your side. With your left hand, rattle the coin in the can.

Now reach out into the air with your right hand, produce the thumb-palmed coin at your fingertips, hold it up to show it, and say, "Property tax. . . ." Pretend to drop that into the can, thumb-palming it as before while your left hand releases a coin from the slide so it sounds like the one dropped from your right hand. Remove your right hand with its thumb-palmed coin, let your hand fall to your side for a moment, then reach down behind your knee to produce the same coin again. Hold it up to show it and say, "Excise tax. . . ."

Pretend to drop it into the can, really thumb-palming it, while your left hand releases another coin from the slide. Continue in that way, seeming to take a coin from your ear, from beneath your elbow, the heel of your shoe, and so on. Don't rush the productions; pause a little before each one, holding the coin up each time so it can be clearly seen before you pretend to drop it into the can. "Luxury tax . . . income tax . . . *thumb tacks?*"

After you have produced the thumb-palmed coin five or six times, pretending each time to drop it into the can, you really do drop it in. Hold it well above the can and visibly let it fall from your right fingers down into the can. Casually show the full palm side of your hand empty, and then sweep your hand through the air as though catching still another coin, closing your fingers as if they held one. Immediately bring your hand into the top of the can, open your hand as if dropping a coin, and with your left hand release one from the slide.

Drop both hands to your sides as you say, "Anybody could learn to do it—with the help of a little magic." Look out toward some person in the audience. "There's one floating past you, sir. Will you just reach out and close your hand around it?" Hold up the can with your left hand and look directly at the person. "Now throw it back, please." Hold the can still, as though waiting to catch it, and when the person throws the imaginary coin, let one drop from the slide so it clinks loudly into the bottom of the can. "Thank you. There's no use trying to hold out on the tax collector, you know."

Loudly rattle all the coins in the can. Then tip the can to the right and hold your cupped right hand close to it as you slide them all out into your hand. With your left hand, turn the can upright again. Bring your right hand to the top as though dropping all the coins back into the can, but secretly keep about half of them in your right hand. Don't try to palm them or anything; just hold some back in your hand and then let that hand fall to your side with its fingers partly closed around them as your left hand holds up the can and loudly rattles the coins you have dropped into it.

Stop rattling the can and lower your left hand to its side. Say, "As every taxpayer knows, this is called paying through the nose." Bring your right hand, back outward, up to your nose, and bring the can a few inches beneath it with your left hand. Release the coins from the bottom of your right hand, so they shower down into the can. Slap the side of the can with your right hand, put the can on the table, and say, "Thank you all for paying your taxes so promptly. I'll take this over to the tax office right after the show!"

HUSH MONEY

How it looks

You ask to borrow a dollar bill, and when one is offered, you say, "Will you please bring it up, so everybody can help you keep an eye on your money?" Taking the bill from the spectator, you have him stand beside you. "I'll write you an I.O.U. for it," you say, writing it on a small card, and including the serial number. Then you fold his bill, cover it with a handkerchief, and have him hold it.

"Just say 'Go!'" you tell him. When he does, you suddenly pull the handkerchief from his fingers, and the bill has vanished. "You said it—I didn't," you say. "I collect more dollars that way." Putting the handkerchief away in your pocket as though the trick were finished, you pick up a pack of cards, shuffle them, and announce, "Now, for my next trick. . . ."

But then you stop, smile, and put the cards aside. "Since you still have my I.O.U., I suppose I'll have to offer you some hush money," you tell him. "I have some socked away here somewhere." Reaching around under your jacket, you pull an old sock from your hip pocket and hold it up to show it. From inside the sock, you take out a baby's bottle, sealed at the top with its cap and nipple. In the glass bottle, there is a dollar bill, and you point to it and say, "Hush money."

You unscrew the cap of the baby's bottle, remove the bill, and unfold it. "Will you look at the serial number I wrote on the I.O.U.?" You read the number on the bill aloud, while he checks the number on the I.O.U. card he has been holding. "Is that your number?" When he says that it is, you hand him the bill and say, "Then this dollar must be yours."

What you need

A dollar bill

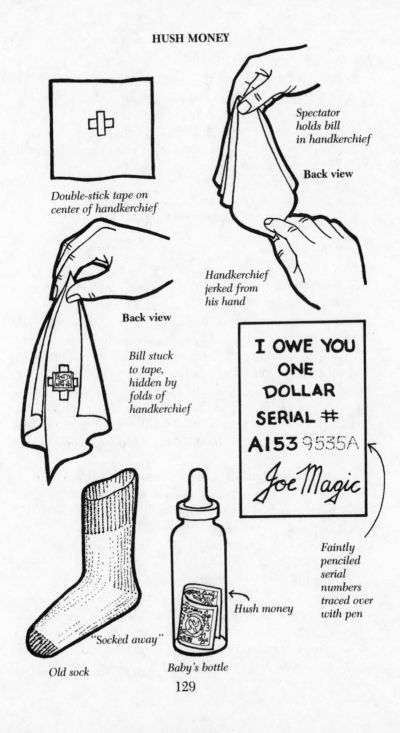

Double-stick tape on center of handkerchief

Spectator holds bill in handkerchief

Back view

Handkerchief jerked from his hand

Back view

Bill stuck to tape, hidden by folds of handkerchief

I OWE YOU ONE DOLLAR SERIAL # A153 9535A

Joe Magic

Faintly penciled serial numbers traced over with pen

"Socked away"

Old sock

Hush money

Baby's bottle

A dark-colored handkerchief or a small table napkin of heavy cloth that cannot be seen through

Double-stick transparent tape, the kind that is sticky on both sides

An old sock, big enough to hold a baby's bottle

A full-size (8 oz.) transparent glass baby's nursing bottle, with screw-cap and nipple

A pack of cards

A plain unruled 3 x 5 inch office index file card

A *broad-tipped* black felt marking pen and a pencil

How you fix it

Spread the handkerchief open on the table. Fasten a 1½-inch length of double-stick tape to the handkerchief at its center, running it across horizontally just beneath the handkerchief's middle fold. Fasten another strip the same length vertically over the first one, so the two form a cross.

Loosely fold the handkerchief in half from top to bottom, again in half from top to bottom, then from left to right, and finally from right to left. Folding it that way puts the proper corner on top, so that when you later pick it up to shake it open the tape will be at the back, hidden from view. (Fresh strips of tape should be used each time you do the trick.)

Turn the file card with its narrow edges top and bottom. At a point about 1½ inches up from the bottom edge, copy the serial number of the dollar bill on the card with the pencil, *lightly* but in fairly large numerals.

Fold the bill horizontally in half from top to bottom, in half from right to left, and again in half from left to right. Put the bill inside the baby's bottle, screw the cap and nipple back on the bottle, and put the bottle into the sock.

Put the file card into the right inside pocket of your jacket, written side of the card toward your body, and clip the broad-tipped pen into the same pocket. Stuff the sock with the bottle in it into your right hip pocket, with the top of the sock hanging out so you can reach it easily, but not so it hangs in view beneath the edge of your jacket. Have the pack of cards and the handkerchief, folded so the proper corner is on top, on the table you will use when performing.

What you do

Ask to borrow a dollar bill and invite the spectator to bring it up "so everybody can help you keep an eye on your money." Have him stand to your right, in front of the table. Take the bill from him, hold it up to show it, snap it between your fingers, and say, "This looks like a good one."

Handling the bill gives you a chance to deliberately turn it face down, so George Washington's picture and the serial numbers are facing away from you. Hold the bill that way in your right hand and say, "I'll write you an I.O.U. for it."

Turn so you are facing the spectator. With your left hand, reach into your inner jacket pocket and remove the pen and the card, keeping the card upright and with its face toward you. Hold the card against the palm of your upright left hand, thumb across it near the top, and place the bill there, to hold it at the top of the card with your thumb.

Say the words aloud as you print them on the card with the pen, "I.O.U. one dollar. Serial number ..." Glance at the bill, "discover" that it is face down, and turn it over, face up, to hold it again under your thumb so you can read the serial numbers on it. This is an important bit of business that helps convince the spectators you are really reading the numbers from the bill as you pretend to copy them.

Look at the numbers on the bill, but ignore them, and say aloud the first few numbers that are already lightly penciled on the card as you mark right over them with the broad-tipped pen, which covers up the pencil marks, "A 153..." Glance up at the bill again, as if copying the numbers from that, and trace over the rest of your penciled numbers, saying, "... 45353 A" (or whatever your numbers happen to be). Take your time as you go along to make sure the thick pen strokes cover all the penciling. Then sign your name at the bottom of the card and hand it to the spectator. Put the pen away in your pocket.

Fold the bill from top to bottom, then right to left and left to right. Hold up the folded bill with your left hand, between your upright thumb and fingertips. With your right hand, pick up the top corner of the handkerchief that is on the table and shake the handkerchief open. Drape it over your left hand so the center of it covers your fingers and the bill.

Bring your right hand to the outside top of the handkerchief to grip the bill through the cloth. Press the center of the handkerchief to it firmly so the sticky tape underneath is fastened to the bill. Lift the handkerchief and bill away with your right hand. Show your left hand empty and, with your right hand, hold out the handkerchief to the spectator as you say, "Will you hold it, please?"

Give him the top of it so he can hold the folded bill through the handkerchief and take your hand away. Have him hold it up high and then tell him, "Just say 'Go!'"

When he does, grip a corner hanging down at the *back* of the handkerchief with your right hand, and with a sudden snap pull the handkerchief straight down out of his hand. This leaves the bill, stuck to the tape, hidden inside the folds of the handkerchief as it hangs down from your right hand. The bill seems to have vanished. Tell the spectator, "You said it—I didn't. . . . I collect more dollars that way."

Gather up the handkerchief with the bill hidden inside it, take it with your right hand, and stuff it into your right-hand jacket pocket to leave it there. As though the trick were over and you intended to keep his vanished dollar bill, pick up the pack of cards, start shuffling them, and announce, "For my next trick. . . ."

Look at the spectator, smile, shake your head and put the cards back on the table, and say, "Since you still have my I.O.U., I suppose I'll have to offer you some hush money. I have some socked away here somewhere."

Reach under your jacket and take the sock from your hip pocket. Hold it up by the top to give the audience a chance to see what it is, and laugh. Then take the baby's bottle out of it, hold that a moment, and slowly tilt the bottle back and forth so the bill can be seen inside it. Point to the bill in the bottle and say, "Hush money."

Unscrew the cap and put it on the table with the sock. Let it be seen that your hands are empty and tip the mouth of the bottle toward you so you can get your fingers into it to remove the bill. Open out the bill, hold it up and snap it between your hands, and ask the spectator, "Will you look at the serial number on the I.O.U. I gave you?"

Slowly read aloud the serial number on the bill while he checks it against the number on the card. Ask, "Is that your number?" Hand him the bill and say, "Then this dollar must be yours . . . which means I get back my I.O.U." Take the card from him, thank him, tear up the card, and drop the pieces on the table, as you say, "I'm always glad to clear up my debts."

RAINBOW REPEAT BILLS

This is a colorful new version of a trick magicians know as The Six-Bill Repeat. As it usually is shown, you count six dollar bills singly from hand to hand, discard three of them, and still have six, repeating the process several times. But in this version, although you start with six plain bills and always have six left, the ones you count off are "crazy money," with polka dots, stripes, a recipe, a health warning, and other humorous surprises, including designs in full color, and finally a rainbow.

How it looks

You take out a wallet and remove some dollar bills from it, showing each bill on both sides as you count them singly from hand to hand. "One, two, three, four, five, six dollar bills—all alike, all the same," you say. "That's the trouble

RAINBOW REPEAT BILLS

MAKING THE ENVELOPE BILLS

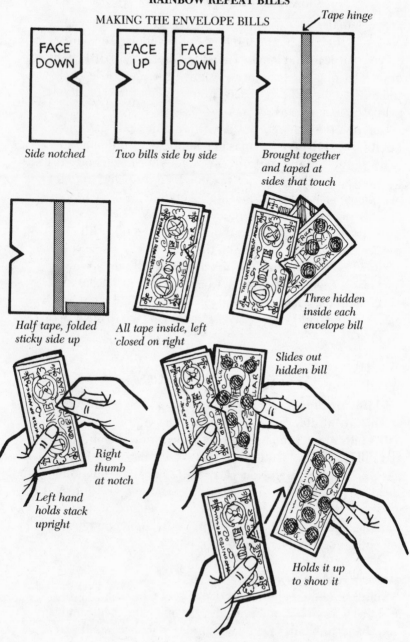

Tape hinge

FACE DOWN

Side notched

FACE UP FACE DOWN

Two bills side by side

Brought together and taped at sides that touch

Half tape, folded sticky side up

All tape inside, left closed on right

Three hidden inside each envelope bill

Left hand holds stack upright

Right thumb at notch

Slides out hidden bill

Holds it up to show it

THE "CRAZY MONEY" BILLS

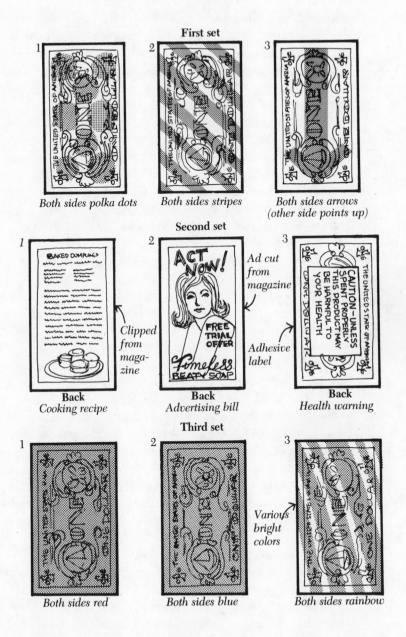

First set

1. *Both sides polka dots*
2. *Both sides stripes*
3. *Both sides arrows (other side points up)*

Second set

1. **Back** *Cooking recipe* — *Clipped from magazine*
2. **Back** *Advertising bill* — *Ad cut from magazine* / *Adhesive label*
3. **Back** *Health warning*

Third set

1. *Both sides red*
2. *Both sides blue*
3. *Both sides rainbow* — *Various bright colors*

with money. It's just plain dull. Always the same old dreary gray and green." You stack the bills together. "Don't get me wrong. I have nothing against money. I like the product— but they could use more imagination in the way they package the stuff. It hasn't changed in years. Why can't we have something different—like polka-dot bills?"

Taking one of the dollars from the top of the stack, you show that it suddenly has big black dots all over it, ten spots on each side. "At least, you could always tell a ten-spot when you had one." Discarding that by dropping it into a small basket on your table, you take another bill from the stack and show that it now has black stripes on both sides. "Or striped money?" You discard that and take a third one, which now has big arrows on each side. "Or money that would point the way—so that whenever you have to pay it out . . . you can tell somebody exactly where to go?"

As you count the remaining bills singly from hand to hand, you say, "But, no—it's always the same old dreary gray and green. . . . One, two, three, four, five, six." Stacking them together, you ask, "Why not use the backs of dollar bills to print useful information?" You take one from the stack and show that the back of it suddenly has some printing on it. "Like this recipe—for banana-lemon pie."

Discarding that, you take another and show an advertisement printed on the back. "Why doesn't the government sell the space for advertising—and use the income to cut taxes?" Taking another, you show a small label on the back of it. "Why not use it for public notices?" You read from the label: " 'Warning. . . . Unless spent properly, this product may be injurious to your health, safety, or peace of mind."

You drop that into the basket. "But, no—it's always the same old dreary gray and green," you repeat as you again count the remaining bills from hand to hand, and still have six. "Our postage stamps are different. Commemoratives for everything from forgotten vice-presidents to National

Pickle Week. All colorful and bright. Why not dollar bills in full color? Red ... or blue ... " You show one that is colored red on both sides, another colored blue, and then discard them. "Or a rainbow. . . . Everybody knows there's a pot of gold at the end of the rainbow." After showing a bill colored like a rainbow, you drop that into the basket.

"But I guess it won't ever happen. It's just wishful thinking. I always wind up with the same old dreary gray and green dollars I started with." You again count aloud as you drop them singly from your hand into the basket, "One, two, three, four, five, six."

What you need
Eighteen play-money bills
A secretary-type wallet or other folder in which to keep the bills flat and in order
A small basket or box, slightly longer and wider than the bills
An old magazine
A self-adhesive label, about 1 x 3 inches
Felt-tip pens, black and assorted colors
Transparent tape
Rubber cement
Scissors, a pencil, and a ruler

How you fix it
There are three envelope-like bills in which other bills are concealed. Start by putting a bill on a table, back up and narrow ends top and bottom. A triangular-shaped notch must be cut in one side to provide an opening for the tip of the thumb.

Put the ruler at the bill's right-hand margin, measure half the length of the bill from top to bottom, and make a pencil dot on the margin at that point. Make a second dot ½ inch up from that and a third dot ½ inch down from the original one. Then measure ¾ inch in from the original dot toward the center of the bill and make a dot there. Draw pencil lines from that to the upper and lower dots on the margin, and cut out the triangular piece inside the pencil lines.

Turn that bill *face up*, with the notch you just cut toward the left. Place a second bill *face down* to the right of it. Bring the two together side by side, so their inner long edges touch and the bills are exactly even at the top and bottom. Hinge them together that way by running a vertical strip of tape down the middle from top to bottom, overlapping both bills.

Attach *half the width* of another strip of tape horizontally to the bottom edge of the right-hand bill. Fold the unattached half of that strip up upon itself, sticky side up, and make sure none of it is below the bill's bottom edge.

Now close the left-hand bill down upon the right-hand one, as though closing a book, and press the taped edges together to flatten them. All the tape should be at the inside, with none showing. The result is a double bill, open at the top and right sides, with a triangular notch at the center of the right side of the upper one. From front and back, it looks like a single bill. You will need two more of those, made the same way.

Here is how the various "crazy money" bills are made:

Polka Dots: Turn a bill with its back up, narrow ends top and bottom, and pencil ten circles on it, each the size of a quarter. Space them out so they look like the two fives on a pair of dice: two dots side by side, a single one, two more side by side, and so on, so the audience will see at a glance that there are ten. Keep all the circles within the borders of the bill's printed designs, leaving the outer margins plain. Then fill in the circles with the black pen, turn the bill over face up, and make ten similar dots on that side.

Stripes: Again, keep within the borders of the bill's printed designs, leaving the margins plain. There are four slanted horizontal stripes, each about ½ inch wide, across the back of the bill, and four more across the face. Make them by ruling off parallel pairs of slanted pencil lines, and then filling them in with the black pen.

Arrows: Pencil a large vertical arrow, pointing down from top to bottom, on the back of a bill by drawing parallel lines about ½ inch apart. Draw another arrow pointing up on the face of the bill. Fill them both in with the black pen.

Recipe: Look through the old magazine and find a column of printed text that will fit vertically within the borders of the back of a bill. The audience won't be able to read it, but you want something without headlines, with solid text, that somewhat resembles a printed recipe. Cut it out and rubber-cement it to the back of a bill.

Advertising Bill: In the magazine, find an advertisement, or part of one, that has some large, simple design or illustration with a few big words. It should be something immediately recognized from a distance as an advertisement, of a size to fit within the borders of the bill, and in plain black and white so as not to spoil the later surprise of the colored bills. Clip it out and rubber-cement it vertically to the back of a bill.

Health Warning: Use a typewriter if you can, or otherwise the black pen, and type or print the following on the self-adhesive label: "Warning: Unless spent properly, this product may be injurious to your health, safety, or peace of mind." Turn a bill back upward, long edges top and bottom, and attach the label to it. Although the audience won't be able to read the words, it should look like a warning label when you show it and read it aloud.

Red and Blue Bills: With colored pens, color the face and back of one bill all red and another all blue. Color them solidly, but so that the designs of the bills faintly show through the coloring, keeping within the borders and leaving the margins plain.

Rainbow Bill: The face and back of this, within the borders, should be filled with curving bands of bright contrasting colors, arched like a rainbow. Turn a bill with its long edges top and bottom, draw curving parallel lines with a pen of each color, and then fill them in. Such colors as yellow and pink won't show up well, so use more brilliant colors: red, blue, green, orange, purple.

To set everything for the trick, place the *arrows* bill vertically face down on a table, the *stripes* on top of it, and *polka dots* on top of that. Square them up and slide the three together inside one of the face-down envelope bills. Tap the edges so the loose bills are entirely within the double one and no edges show. Put that envelope bill aside, face down on the table.

Now place the *health warning* bill face down, the *advertising* bill on top of it, and the *recipe* on top of that. Slide the three inside a second envelope bill so no edges show, and put it face down on top of the first envelope bill. Then stack the *rainbow* bill face down, the *blue* upon it, and the *red* on that, and slide them into the third envelope bill. Put that face down on top of the other two. The notched edges of all three envelope bills should be toward the right. Put three single bills face down on top of them. Then turn the *entire stack* of bills *face up*.

From the top down, the face-up bills are now stacked in this order: envelope with drawn design bills, envelope with the printed clippings, envelope with the colored bills, three single bills. Put them into the wallet that way and put the wallet into the right-hand inside pocket of your jacket. Have the small basket or box on your table.

What you do

Take out the wallet, remove the stack of face-up bills, and put the wallet aside. Square up the bills and hold them vertically in the palm of your left hand, thumb across the middle of the stack and fingers at the right edge. Deal the top bill from your left hand into the upturned palm of your right hand, as though dealing a card off the top of a pack.

Hold it with the tips of your right fingers against the left edge of the bill and thumb across the middle of it. Turn your right hand out to the right, palm toward the audience, to hold the bill vertically upright and display the face of it as you count aloud, "One . . ."

Bring your right hand back and deal the second bill from your left *on top* of the first one in your right hand. Turn your right hand palm outward as before, to display the second bill, and count aloud, "Two . . ." Continue until you have counted the six from hand to hand. "One, two, three, four, five, six dollar bills . . . all alike, all the same. That's the trouble with money. It's just plain dull. Always the same old gray and green."

You are now holding the six bills upright in your right hand. Put them back into your left hand by turning your right hand palm downward as you naturally would, which turns the entire stack *face down*. You have reversed the original order of the bills by counting them on top of one another from hand to hand. The first of the envelope bills is now on top of the face-down stack with its notched edge toward the right. Square them up and hold the stack vertically upright in your left hand.

"Don't get me wrong. I have nothing against money," you say. "I like the product—but they could use more imagination in the way they package the stuff. It hasn't changed in years."

While you are saying that, put the tip of your right thumb over the notch of the envelope bill. Press lightly on the edge of the first concealed bill, the *polka dots*, and draw it out a little, but don't yet bring it into full view. (There is no need to put your thumb inside the envelope bill; the notch is there so you can avoid doing that. Just slide the concealed bill out to the right, to take the edge of it between your thumb and fingertips.)

"Why can't we have something different—like polka-dot bills?" Hold up the spotted bill with your right hand, give the audience a moment to realize that one of the bills you previously showed plain has suddenly become spotted, and say, "At least you could always tell a ten-spot when you had one." Show it front and back and put it into the small basket on your table. Take the second concealed bill from the top of the stack in your left hand in the same way, show the stripes on the front and back, comment about it, and discard that in the basket. Finally show the bill with the arrows and put that in the basket.

That leaves an empty envelope bill on top of the stack in your left hand. Take that one with your right hand and hold it up to show it, as you say, "But, no—it's always the same old dreary gray and green." Return that one to the *front* of the stack in your left hand, under all the others. (Just remember that when an envelope bill has been emptied, you always hold it up and show it as you remark about all of them being "dreary gray and green," and then put it back under all the rest to get rid of it.)

Now deal the bills singly from your left hand into your upturned right hand, putting them face down one on top of another as you count them aloud: "One, two, three, four, five, six." Then take the whole stack with your left hand and deal them singly into your right hand again in the same way, counting them from hand to hand a second time. But the second time, do it quickly and silently, without saying anything, as if repeating the count merely to confirm that you still have six, as when you started, even though you have discarded three in the basket. When you have finished the second count, put the face-down stack back into your left hand and square up the bills.

The double counting is done to impress the audience with the fact that you have only six bills and also to restack the bills in your left hand so the second envelope bill is now on top. Hold the stack vertically upright in your left hand. With the tip of your right thumb over the notched edge as before, slide out the recipe bill. Hold it up with your right hand to show the plain face of it, then turn it to display the printed clipping attached to the back. Pretend to read from it as you comment that it is a recipe for "banana-lemon pie." Drop it into the basket.

Then bring out the *advertising* bill, show its back, comment about it, and drop that into the basket. Next show the health warning bill, displaying its label on the back and then turning it horizontally so you can read it aloud. Put that into the basket.

Again, that leaves an empty envelope bill on top of the stack, so you hold it up and say, "But, no—it's always the same old dreary gray and green," and to get rid of it you put it back under all the rest. Now count them aloud singly from your left hand to your right hand, then take the whole stack with your left hand and silently repeat the hand-to-hand count, square them up, and hold the stack vertically upright in your left hand.

The third envelope bill is now on top. Follow the routine as given and show first the red bill, then the blue, and finally the rainbow, discarding each in the basket. You are left at the end with three singles and three empty envelope bills, each of which looks like a single bill. "But I guess it won't ever happen. It's just wishful thinking," you say. "I always wind up with the same old dreary gray and green dollars I started with."

Count them slowly from hand to hand, showing both sides of each bill, and drop them singly into the basket. "One, two, three, four, five, six."

INDEX

145